AN UPSTATE BOYHOOD:

World War II and Beyond

by

Thomas O. Kelly II

DORRANCE
PUBLISHING CO
EST. 1920
PITTSBURGH, PENNSYLVANIA 15238

Dorrance Publishing Co
585 Alpha Drive
Pittsburgh, PA 15238
Visit our website at *www.dorrancebookstore.com*

ISBN: 978-1-4809-5717-6
eISBN: 978-1-4809-5740-4

To: Dorothy Louise Schiller Kelly
my very particular "Gift from God"

CONTENTS

INTRODUCTION

> Memoir: "A history or narrative composed from personal
> experiences and memory often, esp. an account of one's
> life ..." *Webster's Collegiate Dictionary*, 5th edition, 1943

A presidential memoir immediately piques curiosity. How was that decision reached? What at that point framed presidential thinking? Who counseled the president? Those and many other questions speak to our desire to understand the world as we find it; and how it emerged.

A personal memoir, on the other hand may describe the world as we find it, but is unlikely to explain it in any meaningful way. Yet a personal memoir will, not infrequently, give us illustrations about the world as it was, and perhaps more frequently, how men and women, boys and girls met that world, engaged it and coped with it. How did they see the world? How did they move through it? What, if anything, did what we now perceive to be world historical events seem like at the moment they occurred?

This memoir deals with a single life, as it was lived between 1935 and 1963 just over a quarter-of-a-century. Yet that brief moment of time includes a reasonable chunk of the Great Depression, World War II, the inception of the Cold War, the Korean War, the so-called Red Scare and the efforts of Americans in the aftermath of World War II to move toward a more just society in regard to race relations or to resist such efforts. It also saw, driven by the automobile, the creation of a suburban lifestyle and culture. Techno-logical advances and the increasing ubiquity of radio, television and motion pictures created a new mass culture. That, in turn, saw a concomitant weak-ening of local and regional cultures – customs, and accents, mores and folk-lore. It is the era into which I was born, was educated and came to maturity, primarily in Upstate New York, and in urban environments.

My memories, like all memories, are particular. I remember little of the Depression, in that area I am primarily restricted to vignettes. I remember for example, celebrating my mother's birthday with a penny *Baby Ruth* with a candle dug into it. And I still find myself, in economic or financial matters, stamped with the caution of my parents' generation. I have vivid and quite extensive memories of World War II – though primarily, a child's eye view. Some of these memories are, no doubt, common and even banal to some. Others will be surprising, enlightening and even entertaining to many.

Singular events, institutions and individuals (mother, father, schools, war) leaven and affect **all** the memories. Those of school and church. Of the state and practice of medicine. Of communications and entertainment. Of stability and change. Many are shared with more than one generation. In some cases (trolley cars and milk horses) my experiences are very sim-ilar to those of my father's youth. Some memories are societal: the rationing system of World War II. Some are peculiarly individual: parental attitudes toward child rearing and punishment. Though for some they will share sim-ilarities. School days, with their equivalencies and differences will summon comparisons from virtually all generations.

In a world which has established the notion and the phrase "helicopter parents," the life of my youth is bound to seem dangerously improvisa-tional—largely unsupervised, even reckless. Of course, the truth was that we always felt safe and rarely tested ourselves beyond our current abilities. Nonetheless, it was the world as it was, not just for me but for my contem-poraries as a whole. One does suspect that teaching a five or six-year-old boy how to slaughter chickens, in today's world would be a socially dan-gerous task. In 1941-42, it was simple and matter-of-fact.

The world was changing under our feet throughout the period. Sometimes we were aware, other times oblivious. But it was our world and if it was changing, so were we. Some changes simply happened due to *developments* in knowledge and technology. They were not planned but like Topsy, in *Uncle Tom's Cabin* were not so much born or initiated, they "just growed." Others represented a challenge to the *status quo,* which some embraced and others resisted.

It all represented a singular view of the middle-third of the 20th Century – and I was there. Whether I was, in some sense a nobody, or at some level an Everyman, the reader can decide. I only hope that the reading experience will, at some level, communicate a trifle of the gusto with which that life was lived.

Author's Notes

The reminiscences found within this memoir are accurate to the best of my recollection and belief. Statistics relevant to specific historical or physical phenomena (e.g., casualties during "The Blitz" or snowfall in Syracuse, NY, in the 1940s have been culled from standard reference sources.

Odd as it may seem, I actually do recall all the names of the nuns who taught me at the Cathedral Academy in Syracuse between Sept. 1940 and Sept. 1946. Perhaps it was constancy of association, perhaps they were particularly talented teachers or merely powerful personalities.

Obviously, no one is likely to recall the names of all the individuals with whom he has associated over a period of nearly thirty years. To spare the reader who might wonder which names are real and which have merely been assigned, more or less arbitrarily, those assigned are indicated by some form of use of the word "call."

The chronology of the story is also largely, though not precisely correct. In all cases, at a minimum, the order of events is accurate or nearly so.

CHAPTER 1
Upstate/Downstate

In the early 1950s, the Iona College basketball team (New Rochelle, NY) went to Philadelphia to play a basketball game. In the aftermath, an Iona undergraduate entered the Philadelphia railroad station, went to the ticket window and said, "May I have a ticket to the City." The ticket agent, annoyed, said: "You New Yorkers are all alike." The student, who was from Queens, responded, "Yeah, but you knew where I wanted to go, didn't you?" Thus spoke the quintessential, "imperial New Yorker": i.e., a denizen of New York City.

But, is/was he a New Yorker in a universal sense? Probably not, but he was in the imperial sense to which I refer. New York City in a precise sense consists of five boroughs or counties: Manhattan, Bronx, Brooklyn, Staten Island and Queens (officially, New York, Bronx, Kings, Richmond and Queens). Then there is the area often socially and politically defined as the New York Metropolitan Area. Note that the word "City" has already disappeared. That area includes Nassau and Suffolk Counties (Long Island) and the Northern suburbs and exurbs: Westchester, Rockland and Putnam counties, as well as portions of Duchess, Orange and Ulster counties. That leaves **forty-nine** counties of the sixty two in New York State which are virtually never included in descriptions of what is universally now referred to as *"**The Big Apple.**"* Those counties, which frequently have little in com-

1

mon and often would prefer not to be lumped together, are, willy-nilly, usually referred to as *"Upstate."* Their inhabitants are sometimes referred to, in what was originally a New York City term of derision directed at unsophisticated country folk, as *"Apple Knockers."* Indeed, residents of Upstate to some degree, share the feeling of pre-Civil War North Carolinians who often said (re Virginia and South Carolina) that North Carolina "was a valley of humility located between two mountains of arrogance."

It appears that the great majority of the American people are, consciously or otherwise, in agreement with the definitions of my "Imperial" New Yorker. If you say, "I am a New Yorker" or "I'm from New York" virtually anywhere in the world, the immediate assumption is that you live in or very near New York City. Well, I am a New Yorker – but I approach this as a member of the 49 counties. I was, if you will, born and raised an "apple knocker," though I went to college in the New York Metropolitan area, where I met and married my wife Dorothy and where our three oldest children were born. I did my graduate study at Fordham University in the Bronx and, to abuse a battered cliché, "some of my best friends are New Yorkers."

The story I have to tell is about an apple knocker, now in his 80s, who was born, reared and educated through high school in various parts of Upstate New York in the 20th Century. My experiences are likely to have been quite different from those of my contemporaries who were raised in "The City" (for example I never heard of a "chocolate egg cream" until I went to college, a fact that I very much regret). It is probably correct to say that, in my childhood "Upstate" was more parochial or provincial than it is today. Memories of visits to my aunts, uncles and cousins in "the City" did suggest, however, that there was, perhaps, nearly as much that was provincial in the Bronx as there was in Syracuse.

I was actually born in the suburbs. The suburb was Mineville, the "urb" was Port Henry, Essex County, New York - which is roughly 3.3 degrees of latitude north of Manhattan and in 1935, as in 2016, a world apart economically and culturally. Many of the mine workers' houses in Mineville would not get indoor plumbing until after World War II. Both Port Henry and Mineville can be located on a road map as existing within the "Blue Line" – the phrase which defines those portions of the Adirondack Mountain region which are subject to the New York State Constitution's constraints under the description, "Forever Wild." Those constraints have limited development of the region for more than a century. It would be reasonable to suggest that "Forever Wild" has been beneficial to the state and an ecological triumph. It would be equally reasonable to suggest that it has driven residents from their homes and witnessed the decay of job producing economic activity.

I am the son of Thomas O'Connor Kelly and Helen Cecile Kane. He was born in 1906 in Pennsylvania and she, in 1911 in New York City, to which her father had immigrated from Kells, in County Meath in Ireland. As the names would tend to indicate, both parents were of Irish descent and both were Roman Catholic. As I remember the family stories, my father had even, briefly, entered an Augustinian seminary to study for the priesthood. I suspect the key word in that story is "briefly." They married in the summer of 1934 and I was born in August of 1935 – indeed on the 13th day of the month. Two days later, the great American humorist, Will Rogers was killed in a plane crash. It is a measure of Rogers' popularity and the innocence of that time, that the authorities in the "lying in" hospital where my mother was recuperating from childbirth, decided not to tell the new mothers, lest it be too upsetting for them. My mother always found that decision to be amusing. It probably should be noted here that in that era women were often hospitalized for up to ten days after childbirth to recover their strength. It was one of the few amusing elements of my birth. My mother was a very small woman, about 5' tall and I think virtually never over 100 pounds, and I was a very big baby (over 9 pounds, I am told). The attending physician, she later told me, relied much more on forceps and force than upon finesse.

I was born in Port Henry because at that moment my parents were visiting my paternal grandparents who lived there. Our home was in Syracuse, NY, in Onondaga County. Relatively soon after my birth I was ensconced in a wicker basket, placed (unrestrained) on the back seat of the family car and transported to Syracuse where I would pass my so-called formative years, until about 1947, when we would move to Buffalo in Erie County.

My father, at this time, was a traveling salesman who sold coal and coke to industrial and commercial accounts. Though these were Depression years, he did well. In 1937 or early 1938, my mother gave birth to my sister, also named Helen Cecile but called "Keenie." My memories of her are few though apparently we enjoyed one another. One story which I recall involves the notion that I (we shared a bedroom) was either keeping her awake or waking her up during the night. I no longer recall which, but one parent felt I was the culprit and the other disagreed. To solve the puzzle they decided to watch us to see what happened. They found Keenie calling to me in baby talk until I awakened. I then "rode" the crib until we were in close proximity. I have no idea as to whether we engaged in philosophical discussions, or just played gin.

Keenie apparently adored my father. I remember my mother telling me that she would be feeding her in her high chair with all going well until his car pulled into the driveway. With that, the baby knocked the bowl off the tray of the chair, brushed aside the spoon and demanded her father's attention. We were, by all accounts, a happy and prosperous family.

Shortly after my birth, in 1936, my grandfather, my father's father, died, and my grandmother (Nan) came to live in Syracuse with my father's twin brother Joe, and my Aunts, Margie and Joan. Sunday dinner at Nan's formed a regular, almost ritualistic portion of my boyhood. My mother had been orphaned before she was ten, when her parents Terrence and Ellen Kane died in 1918 and 1919. That was, of course, the time of the so-called Spanish Flu.

In the spring of 1939, Keenie contracted Whooping Cough followed by pneumonia and died. She was "waked" at home, and I think my only really clear memory of her is of her in a sprigged dress, lying in her coffin.

It was also the earliest confrontation I remember with my father. He insisted that I kiss her, lying in her coffin. I demurred.

My mother, who would have no other children, was, as she always would be, stoic. Her consolations would always be the idea that "God has His reasons" and "He would send you no burden you could not bear." As was common with that generation of Catholics, and many of the next, she would "offer it up." Offering it up meant trying to join one's own suffering to that of Christ on the Cross, for the good of humanity.

She also decided that I needed to go to school. I think she thought that I was now an only child and needed to have regular contact with other children – which was no longer possible at home. Since Keenie died in March, and I only turned four in August, that posed some administrative problems. Then, as now, children started kindergarten at age five. The challenge she set herself was a daunting one. Indeed, in our time it would have been impossible. However, she knew her son to be "exceedingly bright" and "highly talented" and saw no reason why administrative rules should form any impediment to her wishes. In any event, she went to the parish school, St. Vincent de Paul, and somehow convinced (browbeat?) either the nun who was the principal or the priest who was the pastor, and just after my fourth birthday Thomas O'Connor Kelly II started school. I have few memories of that year, though unusually for a Catholic school in that time and place, my teacher was a laywoman and not a nun. At the end of the school year, my mother was told that while I had done very well academically, the school thought that socially I should repeat the year rather than move on to first grade. Having assured herself that the problem was not academic, she determined to ignore the advice.

Helen Kane Kelly was a redoubtable figure and unwilling to be thwarted. Nor did she intend to see her son delayed. In September, I entered First Grade at St. Mary's (Cathedral Academy). I would attend Cathedral from first through sixth, and into the seventh grade.

My years at Cathedral were, by and large, happy ones. The school was staffed and administered by the Sisters of St. Vincent de Paul (the Daughters, sometimes called Sisters, of Charity). They were exceptionally picturesque. Their habits (gowns) were of a shade of blue a bit more somber than royal blue and their wimples (headgear) of brutally starched white linen with the upper layers folded into a sort of gull wing configuration. It was that head-dress that caused them, on occasion, to be called "God's geese." Only their faces were exposed to view. To see a pair of them (they never moved alone in public) moving tranquilly down a street in Syracuse was something of a spectacle, if there is such a thing as a serene spectacle.

The school contained all twelve grades. Standing in the front entrance, the basement was where the lunch room was located. On the first floor, in my school days, at the far right on the end of the building was the first grade, where I was taught by Sister Jean Marie; then the second grade, Sister Anne Marie; and third, presided over by Sister Raphael. Then, back down the hall to the far left, fourth grade, Sister Anne Marie again; fifth, Sister Stanislaus; and sixth, Sister Blanche. Moving to the second floor the pattern was replicated: seventh, eighth and ninth, tenth eleventh and twelfth. The auditorium, stage, etc., occupied the top floor. Before I finished second grade, some members of the senior class would be missing at graduation as they began to enlist right after Pearl Harbor. Obviously, the school was quite small, probably about 300 or so children – I do remember that, since there were so few boys in the upper grades, that the high school could only play six-man football.

During those early years of formal learning, I also began the usual process of social and cultural orientation or inculcation. In addition, I experienced a child's version of World War II.

CHAPTER 2
School, Religion and World War II

During this early period of my life, my family's economic status passed into a state of steep decline. My father's earnings fell from that of the upper middle class or middle class, moving steadily in the direction of poverty or near poverty.

By the early stages of World War II we were, as it was put at that time, "reduced to welfare." In at least one way, however, we were ahead of our time. When, in later years, my children gleefully frolicked in bubble baths made with powdered soap (*Mr. Bubble?*), I was reminded that once-upon-a-time, I too bathed from a box – though mine was labeled *Rinso* or *Duz* and was intended for clothes or dishes. In that period, probably due to our "reduced circumstances," my mother was absolutely draconic about cleanliness. "Cleanliness was next to Godliness," and poverty was no excuse for appearing to be slovenly – and soap was soap! As our income and social status waned, my father's drinking waxed. I have never known the whys and wherefores. His generation had come of age during prohibition and was a hard-drinking one. I think, too, that my sister's death may well have had a near traumatic impact on him. In those years, also, my mother began to display the first signs of the brain tumor that would lead to her death at 40. He and I were never close, nor were we ever enemies. His life was never an easy one and, in general, his burdens proved to be too much for him. He, too, would die young, at 60.

In retrospect, his burdens were enormous. Before Pearl Harbor, my mother had begun to display the symptoms of her fatal disease. Slowly, but persistently, her symptoms became more serious. One quite frightening manifestation was the irregular appearance of what seemed to be *grand mal* epileptic seizures, though limited to one side of the body. They led to false diagnoses of epilepsy. A neurologist in Syracuse, perhaps as early as 1942, told her, "Mrs. Kelly, you have a brain tumor, and I hope you do not have to die to prove me right." There would also be a number of exploratory operations which often left her, until her hair grew back, with horseshoe shaped scars on her temple. Nothing was ever found. I have always assumed that, by the standards of the day, even had something been found, it probably would have been inoperable. Displaying her characteristic strength and humor, she pressed on. I can remember her saying, with a glint in her eye, that she was grateful that the turban had returned to style, because turbans disguised the shortness or absence of her hair after an operation, or hid the scar. Her illness and I sort of grew up together through the years. The result was that I became to some degree not only her child, but her confidante. It certainly, especially in its later stages, imposed some restrictions upon me, but it also, I think, rather force-fed me into a relatively early maturity.

As our income declined, we fairly regularly found ourselves moving to increasingly unprepossessing quarters. My first memories of our home are of a house on the outskirts of a then nearly somnolent Syracuse University campus. It was, at that time, not the frenzied giant it would become in the wake of World War II and the coming of the GI Bill. By the time we left Syracuse, in 1947, we were living in the upper flat of a small two-story frame house with no central heating. If one has ever spent a winter in central New York, one has a fully developed view of the virtues of central heating and a very real appreciation of the vicissitudes caused by its absence.

The War – Pearl Harbor

I entered Cathedral Academy (St. Mary's) in the first grade, in September of 1940; I was five years old. By that time, the German Army had conquered

8

Poland, defeated and occupied Denmark and Norway, and overrun Holland, Belgium, Luxembourg and France. The aerial Battle of Britain was just coming to an end, to be succeeded by the *Blitz*: that protracted series of nightly air raids on London and other metropolitan centers, which began on September 7 and ended on May 10, 1941. While many raids were larger, the city averaged 150+ bombers each night. From September 7 to November 11, it was bombed every night but one (64 nights out of 65). Many residents retreated to the subway platforms each night in search of shelter. By May 10, some 30,000 Londoners had died and at least another 25,000 had been treated in hospital emergency rooms for their wounds.

America was still at peace, but the National Guard was called to active duty in the fall of 1940, and the first men to be drafted (*selectees* as they were then called) were scheduled to report just after the first of the year. I was, of course, not aware of this on any philosophical or world historical level, but we were all aware of at least some of it on a personal level. In my case I still vividly remember seeing newsreel footage of the *Blitz*, with London firemen battling the flames as walls crumbled and fell close to them. (Even then, I was an avid movie goer.) I also knew that my Uncle Joe, my father's twin brother, who would turn 35 in 1941, was one of the earliest selectees. Dating from this period as well is one of my earliest surviving photographs. It shows a small boy, fully uniformed. Or, as we said at the time, "wearing his soldier suit." Fashion had begun, at almost all levels, to find fascination in *militaria*.

"Change she was a-comin'." At a more cosmic level, the larger world in which I lived was shifting. Both the United States and American Catholicism were on the cusp of entering a triumphalist era. In each case, it would be of short duration, perhaps about a quarter of a century. It would, however, form cultural patterns that still resonate (though perhaps with a continually diminishing number of people).

In any event, in the next year or so we would find new causes and new slogans entering our young lives. One such was **Bundles for Britain**. The concept of a New York City society woman, its goal was to supply warm

9

clothing and other necessities for beleaguered Englishmen and women. American women would knit garments or afghans, or go through their household's wardrobes to find usable warm clothing: winter coats, knit hats, and so forth. It would then be donated. There were many other groups, some more important, but ***Bundles for Britain***, perhaps because the idea was so simple and neighborly (and alliterative), became the significant, symbolic cause. I think I remember seeing collection boxes in the lobby of movie theatres.

Our everyday existence was not yet totally defined by the war, and many people and events made lasting childhood impressions. In our apartment building, there was a superintendent called Bush. He and his wife were lovely people, who were known to me, as were all adults, as Mr. and Mrs. Bush. They were older than my parents, though perhaps not yet old enough to be grandparents. They were originally farmers, who, I now assume, had probably been driven off their land by the Depression. Mrs. Bush made what I still believe to be the best cookies I have ever tasted. In passing, I should probably note that my mother, whom I believe to be one of the most intelligent and witty women whom I have ever met, was a terrible cook. I have often said to friends that she never baked a cake which did not come out of the oven on a bias. My friends will say, "Well, perhaps it was the oven?" to which I respond, "In five different houses?" Mr. Bush would, on occasion, take me out into the countryside (I assume to where he had formerly had his farm) and we would return after a few hours with produce and, often, poultry, still alive. I was at this time perhaps six or seven years old. We would then, in the course of the next day or two, kill and pluck the chickens and prepare them for cooking. I cannot imagine how modern parents would react to the notion that their small boy was in the basement of their apartment building with the "super," being instructed in how to kill chickens. It was, actually, all very matter of fact. There was, if I may be forgiven the pun, no cackling (diabolical or otherwise), and we ended up with meat on the table. I may not be the best witness, but I do not believe that I was either psychologically scarred or emotionally traumatized. I enjoyed the Bushes and fondly remember the time they devoted to me, perhaps particularly, the cookies. By the time we moved away, I remember that their son, who was in the Army Air Corps, was stationed in China.

I do not think that I was aware of the Second World War itself prior to Pearl Harbor. I do remember my mother speaking frequently of "poor little Finland," which I now know referred to the Soviet Union's assault on Finland in the fall of 1939 and the so-called "Winter War" between Finland and the USSR, 1939-1940. Though something of a military sideshow between the start of World War II, with the invasion of Poland in 1939, and the German *blitzkrieg* into the low countries and France in May of 1940, most Americans very much sympathized with Finland because of the size differential and because the Finns, unlike most European countries, had paid their war debts after World War I.

"Remember Pearl Harbor" was then the slogan, and I do. We were living in an apartment on East Genesee Street at the time. Directly across from our front windows was a movie theatre (which I patronized as frequently as I was allowed). On that Sunday afternoon, we had not gone to my grandmother's house for dinner, and my mother and father were reading and talking. I heard an unusual noise and went to the window to see what it was. Under the marquee of the theatre I saw a newspaper boy (I think there were no newspaper girls in Syracuse in 1941) waving a newspaper and shouting, "EXTRA, EXTRA!" A sight and sound which I had never experienced before and have never experienced since. My father went downstairs and across the street, bought a paper and we learned about Pearl Harbor. My parents turned on the radio to keep up with whatever bulletins came in. From that time on, the war colored virtually all activities: school, entertainment, family, even our toys and games.

During the war itself my father worked as a line inspector at New Process Gear in Syracuse. New Process Gear manufactured the transmissions for huge numbers of cars, jeeps and trucks during the war. The plant, as so many others, worked three shifts around the clock to keep up with the incessant demand made by the armed forces, as well as for lend-lease vehicles for our various allies. At one point, he did become quite alarmed when his local draft board reclassified him into a category which made it highly likely that he would be called into service. My mother's neurologist made representations to the draft board with regard to her medical condition as well as the fact that should she be incapacitated, there would be no one to act as caregiver for me (then 7 or 8 years old). The board thereupon again reclassified him and life returned to what was normal for us.

Newly enrolled at Cathedral, I followed the prescribed curriculum for a first grader, which primarily constituted the "three R's" – Reading, Writing and Arithmetic – though I do believe that I already knew how to read. Since Cathedral was a Catholic school, there was also a fourth "R," Religion. Outward signs of Catholicity were actually commonplace in those days. Most children, by second or third grade, placed some religious sign or symbol on all their school papers. In the top center of each page, for example, they would write or print JMJ [Jesus, Mary and Joseph] or AMDG [ad majorem Dei gloriam – to the greater glory of God]. I don't recall it as a requirement; in fact I don't think I ever did it, but it was normal or customary. In a similar way, as a bus drove down a street, past a Catholic Church, the Catholic men on the bus would momentarily doff their hats as they passed the front of the church out of respect for the "Real Presence" of Christ in the tabernacle. In today's world, where such beliefs are faded if not gone, such customs have died out but at that time they still flourished. In 1940, in the first grade we were either introduced to, or prepared for, the then famous *Baltimore Catechism*. Some form of this guide to Roman Catholicism was used in all Catholic schools at least up to the time of the Second Vatican Council in 1962. The catechism had been prepared by order of the third council of American Bishops at Baltimore in 1885, and it underwent a number of editions. I assume, of chronological necessity, we were using the 1933 edition. I remember, with startling clarity, its opening, which was a question and answer format:

"Who made you?"

"God made me."

"Why did God make you?"

"God made me to know Him, to Love Him, and to serve Him in this world and to be happy with Him forever in the next."

Each day began with prayers and the Pledge of Allegiance to the flag. We all stood for the pledge with our right arms extended toward the flag. If I remember correctly, which is certainly not a given, after the United States entered the war, this was deemed to be too much akin to the *fascist* salute and we began to hold our right hands over our heart. I think we also included the words "under God," which would not become a universal usage until the 1950s. We were taught a robust patriotism which, though intensified by wartime propaganda, was, at root, a part of the Catholic triumphalism to which I have previously referred. The American Catholic Church had begun to feel itself accepted as a part of the fabric of America and of American nationalism. In that context, the role of Hollywood should not be underestimated. The growth of urban themed motion pictures in the 1930s and thereafter gave a portrayal of a more heterogeneous American population with an increasing number of ethnic and urban types, many of which were at least arguably likely to be Catholic. Some films, like *Boys Town* and *Angels With Dirty Faces* focused on specifically Catholic themes or figures. Oddly enough, the star was usually a Catholic such as James Cagney, Pat O'Brien or Spencer Tracy. The 1940s would increase that reality, not only with clearly Catholic films, such as *Going My Way* but also with a plethora of heroic Catholic chaplains in the war films of the era. American Catholic (parochial) schools were also flourishing like the proverbial "green bay tree" in the '40s and '50s.

I almost surely discovered my ambition to become a historian while I was in the first grade – if I did not already know it. The story goes like this. My class was to be given a treat. We were to go to the auditorium to watch a play or a recital being put on by one of the higher grades. I had committed an offence which had alienated Sr. Jean Marie. For my sins, I was to be denied the treat and was, instead, hustled across the hall to sit in with the fourth grade until my classmates returned. As my friends trooped off, I was installed in a seat directly in front of the fourth grade teacher's desk (Sr. Anne Marie). That day, at that time, Sister was teaching them Longfellow's *The Midnight Ride of Paul Revere.* She began by reciting a goodly portion of the poem and then explaining its background. The supposedly sad and suffering little boy was ecstatic. I had discovered that I loved narrative poetry and, more importantly, I was fascinated with the American Revolution. When restored to my classroom, I displayed the requisite penitence, but it had been enormous fun.

Portions of my school days would now be considered unusual. For example, in 1940 and for decades thereafter, parochial school students did not have access to school buses due to then current interpretations of "separation of church and state." Since I lived a considerable distance from Cathedral, every morning (at age 5) I waited with my nickel, for the public bus to arrive at the corner and rode the bus to school. I am sure that the first morning or two my mother made sure that the bus driver was aware of my existence and my destination. In the afternoon, I left school, crossed the street and waited for the bus to complete my round trip. I had, on this leg of the trip, a "perk." The building on that corner had a low, pipe fence or railing. I have no precise recollection of the height of that railing, but I do know that it was just the right height for a small boy to hang by his knees and swing while he waited for the bus.

Corporal punishment was still an accepted practice in public, as well as parochial and private, schools in those days, and I did not entirely escape it. I have no horror stories of sadistic nuns to tell – though some of the sisters were not without imagination. When I was in second grade, Sister Anne Marie (no longer teaching fourth grade) found me wanting in some form of deportment and required me to sit in the waste paper basket for some period of time. It was, of course, a form of shaming as well as punishment. It also lingered a bit because even a short time with a fairly small boy resulted in restricting the circulation of blood to the legs. Either I reformed or she reconsidered the practice because I don't think it ever happened again, certainly not to me. My only other marginally colorful tale of crime and punishment came in the sixth grade. I had become annoyed on the playground at lunch and had said "Hell" or perhaps "Hell's Bells" (a favorite of my father's). Sister Blanche had heard me and decided that I had to be corrected. She called me to the front of the room and ordered me to bite off a chunk of a bar of *Fels-Naptha* soap. (*Fels-Naptha* was a brown, industrial strength soap used for janitorial purposes and was very strong). It tasted horrible and lingered upon the palate. I was fond of Sister but felt myself badly used since I knew that "Hell" was, at worst, a matter of dubious taste as opposed to blasphemous or obscene.

The other side of that coin may be illustrated in a small detail of everyday life. I was probably in second or third grade and I had forgotten my lunch. I was sitting on the steps contemplating an afternoon of fasting, when one of the nuns (I no longer remember which) approached me to see why I was not downstairs in the lunchroom. I explained my circumstances and she said, "Come with me." We then exited school and headed next door to the convent where the other teachers were at lunch. I came very close to panic. Was it her intention to bring me to lunch with the nuns? I could think of little that would scare me more than lunching under the eyes of the entire faculty (except for those supervising the lunchroom). To my great relief, we entered the kitchen where she made me a peanut butter and jelly sandwich and sent me off to the lunchroom to eat. In its own way, this was far more typical of my day to day experience than the incident of the *Fels-Naptha* soap … and far more palatable!

As I approached the second grade, my age created a problem. Catholic children normally made their First Confession and First Communion in second grade because that was when they turned seven years old. The Roman Catholic Church had established seven as the attainment of "the age of reason," which was to say that the children could be presumed to understand the difference between right and wrong. It was also assumed that they would have an appropriate understanding of the solemnity of the religious rite and ritual that they were undergoing. Tommy Kelly, on the other hand, entered second grade at barely six years of age – what to do? Consultations were held, which I assume must have involved at least one priest from the Cathedral. In any event, I was allowed to continue with preparation for the sacraments and, in May, age 6, I made my First Communion.

In our own time, when Confession has become Reconciliation, First Confession/ Reconciliation is sometimes (fairly often) postponed to avoid the possibility of traumatizing children. When I was six, preparing for my First Communion, I was more than well aware that i was capable of offending both God and man and delighted with the prospect of forgiveness and absolution. To the best of my knowledge, we all were. I think most little boys of the era were well aware of their penchant for mischief. My grandmother ("Nan") even used to sing a song to me which both acknowledged the concept and provided some sympathy:

Freckles was his name,
He always used to get the blame
For every broken window-pane.
Oh how they yanked him
Oh how they spanked him.
Freckles was his name.

And, yes, I did have more than an average supply of freckles.

I don't think we were harder or more callous than modern children. I do think we had a much less developed sense of entitlement. Most importantly in this context, Confession was a necessary preparation and preliminary for the reception of the Eucharist in First Holy Communion. Communion, for Roman Catholics is the *actual* reception of the Body and Blood of Christ – not symbolically but actually. That was and is an awe-inspiring belief which is central to Catholicism. It was why our fathers and uncles removed their hats. The nuns of course taught us our catechism and prepared us for the actual ritual in elaborate detail. As we processed down the aisle, our hands were to be joined in a prayerful attitude, fingers pointing upward ("point them in the direction in which you wish to go" – i.e., Heaven or Hell). The ceremony itself, with all the girls clad completely in virginal white and the boys in white trousers and shirts and ties (some with suit jackets – also white), was for all of us a very big deal. It was the first solemn ritual in which we had ever consciously participated. We were feted, received presents and were made much of. In both the spiritual and temporal realms, it was a big day.

Sister Raphael presided over the third grade. I remember her as a pleasant personality, slow to anger and of good humor. In the New York State social studies curriculum of that day, the third grade emphasized the role of various regions of New York in the overall economy of the state. Thus, Buffalo was noted for flour milling and the production of steel, as well as for its role as a Great Lakes port. Rochester was famed for the role played by the Kodak Corporation. Glass was manufactured in Corning, and in Schenectady, the American Locomotive Company and the power generation manufacturing of General Electric led to the slogan, "The City that lights and hauls the world." New York City, in its turn, boasted of the garment district and the Stock Market. It was a comprehensive economic compendium which used a geographic survey as a unifying principal and overview.

It was in the third grade that I most closely approached rebellion, though the spirit was more anarchic than organized. Cathedral Academy was "downtown" in Syracuse. It was at most a few blocks from Cathedral to the main downtown shopping area with its department stores, five and ten cent stores, etc. For reasons now totally unknown to me, a pal and I decided to "ditch" school at lunchtime and go downtown. I do confess that while I no longer remember why, I *was* the instigator. Anyway, we left the school premises without a care in the world. Our first stop was at a local 5 and 10 Cent Store. They had an automatic doughnut making machine and it was customary to place doughnuts which broke in the frying process on the counter as samples. We sampled with gusto until it was made clear to us that our presence was no longer desirable. We then roamed about downtown and rather quickly discovered that downtown actually held little of interest for 7 and 8 year old boys who possessed no appreciable amounts of money. As we became bored, our mental faculties reawakened. We were not in school. Sister Raphael would immediately be aware of that. Action would follow. My mother, at that time, was working in the office of a defense factory, and I knew that I would be home before she returned – but that did not mean that she would not be informed. Boredom began to move into apprehension and apprehension into anxiety. The unalloyed pleasure of rule breaking and its freedom quickly vanished. Well before the school day was over, we had each made our way home.

After my parents confronted and punished me, I moved into the next step of apprehension – what awaited me at school tomorrow. I don't think I slept restfully that night. The next morning, my mother was implacable. I would go to school. I would be punished and I should remember that I richly deserved it. I had inconvenienced many people. I had broken rules. I had disappointed the family.

When I got to school the next morning, Sister Raphael informed me that I was to report to the principal's office. Sister Margaret Mary was, in fact, a lovely woman: gentle and soft spoken. Her hands, however, were very gnarled; perhaps she had arthritis. For some reason, her hands frightened me, and to this day I remember the hands much more than her face or demeanor. She spoke to me in a quiet way, but very firmly. She had sent for Father Ryan (a priest of the parish who was the titular head of the school). He would arrive soon. I would wait in an anteroom. When he arrived, I would formally apologize to him for the disruption I had caused. Then the three of us would walk down the hall to my class where I would make a public apology, first to Sister Raphael and then to my classmates. And so it came to pass. And to this day, more than 70 years later, I have never forgotten it.

In addition to reprimanding naughty boys, Sister Margaret Mary was also concerned with the way we spoke the English language: our native pronunciation. Speech in central New York in those days featured a quite flat, even nasal, pronunciation, most notably in the letter *a*. As was generally true of that era we lacked the universality of the kind of "received" pronunciations that later generations would acquire from radio, motion pictures and television, which has since largely overwhelmed local accents. Under her guidance, Cathedral embarked upon a program to broaden both our speech patterns and our horizons. We were instructed and/or reminded in class, in recitations, any time we opened our mouths that we needed to change. From "My country 'tis of thee, sweet *laaaand* of liberty" we all learned to speak of "sweet lawnd." It certainly sounded odd, indeed affected to us initially, but we soon became accustomed to it and, I think, in many cases, it stuck. As to horizon broadening, we also, at least in my grade, among other things, learned to dance the minuet. I remember learning the steps, bowing to my partner, etc.; all to the tune of Beethoven's *Minuet in G.* There was also a campaign, not I think limited to Cathedral Academy, to stop referring to children as "kids." We were frequently reminded that "kids" were baby goats! That reform was less successful.

Of course, many changes came after December 7, 1941. I was halfway through the second grade when the Japanese attacked. I was between the fifth and sixth grades when the war ended. The war was, as we were so often reminded, emphatically so in the film *Mrs. Miniver,* 1943, a "people's war." In that context, school children were people too. In the three and a half years after Pearl Harbor, the war occupied a central place in American culture. It altered the patterns of all of our lives.

My mother, for example, had never worked outside the home before the war. That phrase itself, *before the war,* and its opposite, *after the war,* speaks clearly to the total centrality of the 1941-1945 historical experience. Most things were now dated by their relationship to the phenomenon of World War II. However, for a time, when her health allowed, even my mother engaged in what was called *war work*. I think that phrase, *war work,* itself, was a comfort to middle-class women who, until after Pearl Harbor, would not have dreamed of "going to business." *War Work* made it all seem so necessary and so temporary – no one then knew how revolutionary it would prove to be. As the demand for women in war production boomed, so did concomitant social problems. Soon every magazine had articles about the problem of "latchkey" children. Latchkey kids were children, often quite young, who would return from school in the afternoon, to an empty house or apartment. The key to the house was often on a string or chain around their neck. They would then be on their own, unsupervised for a number of hours before a parent would return. (When I skipped school in third grade, I was a "latchkey kid.") Thoughtful articles expressed concerns for their well-being and socialization. Issues of juvenile delinquency were regularly raised. With the exception of some child care provided by very large industrial concerns (Kaiser Shipbuilding, e.g.) I recall no significant solutions, and most children seem to have survived reasonably well without becoming a danger to society.

There were, of course, social and physical dangers, as there always are. The coming of penicillin and the sulfa drugs freed parents and children from considerable fear. My own sister's death from whooping cough might have been prevented had she been stricken just a few years later. Few now remember the annual summer parental paroxysm of anxiety as the fear of a polio outbreak mounted. By late summer each year, parents began to limit children's activities, particularly trying to keep them away from movie theatres or other enclosed spaces with significant numbers of people. Polio was a terrible scourge and fear for one's children was a characteristic of the age. I remember going to a hospital to visit a friend of mine who was in an *Iron Lung.* An iron lung was a device which "breathed" for people whose own capacity was limited by paralysis. The patient was supine inside a device which looked something like a boiler laid horizontally. The only view available to the victim was through a mirror mounted at a slight angle just above his or her head. Visitors stood behind or slightly to one side to fit into the viewing space. Throughout, the machine breathed with a heavy "whish/whish" sort of sound. Just to see it was frightening. In retrospect, that visit also illustrated my mother's strength. Few women of the era were willing to expose their children to polio victims, even after the infectious stage had passed.

We were also protected from perceived social dangers. Once when my mother and I were in a drug store, I noticed a small platform perhaps three inches above the floor and measuring about three feet by four feet and covered in small boxes wrapped in plain brown paper. There were no signs or symbols provided. I asked my mother what it was and she told me to wait. Later on I was told about the product known as *Kotex*. When I go to a drug store now and wait for a prescription and see shelves covered for several feet with *KY Jelly* and its knockoffs, I not infrequently think of all those plain brown wrappers. We have certainly "come a long way." Though I am not entirely sure as to what purpose.

Otherwise, life went on with appropriate modifications. For small boys, the old game of Cowboys and Indians gave way to games of "War" against the Nazis and the "Japs." (Now reprehended as racist, "Jap" or even "Nip" was then the common coinage of political leaders, radio commentators and even the *New York Times.*) In our own time we frequently overlook the fact that the heyday of "the greatest generation" was, consciously and unconsciously, quite racist. My mother was a clear proponent of racial equality and would have punished me severely had she ever heard me use what we now call "the N word" – yet she would, quite innocently, if someone told her she could not do something, respond by saying that yes, she could because she was "free, *white* and twenty-one." Similarly, children choosing sides by playing "eeny, meeny, miny moe" in those days, did not catch "*tigers* by the toe." Of course, in some cases, change merely indicated social adjustments. A favorite character, *The Green Hornet,* had a sidekick and general factotum, who was a Japanese man, named Kato. After Pearl Harbor, in a stunning biological metamorphosis, Kato, the Japanese man disappeared and in his place, was Kato, the Filipino.

On a totally personal note let me relate an actual experience of mine during the war years in Syracuse. I was crossing a downtown street, perhaps two or three feet to the right and slightly behind a Negro man (the approved usage of the time) of middle age. He turned his head and spat. Position and wind cause his spittle to land on my coat. He realized almost immediately what had happened and began to apologize in terms so abject that it became embarrassing. It was years later that I realized what had probably occurred. More than likely he had been a member of the **Black Diaspora**, the flight from the South which caused so many people of color to flee North during that period, and probably that was what brought him to Syracuse. If my speculation is correct, such an incident in his youth or early maturity might have resulted in severe punishment. Thus, the level of obsequious apology from an adult to a small boy makes cultural sense – even as it leaves a bad taste in one's mouth.

The emphasis on war was strengthened by a flood of comic books (the concept, or conceit, of the illustrated novel had yet to emerge) thematically focused on war and on the Axis enemy. Familiar figures, such as *Superman* and *Captain Marvel,* increasingly found it necessary to battle the evil Nazis rather than classic villains. In addition, however, old standards were enlivened by new strips such as *The Boy Commandos* and *Captain America,* for whom the Axis were the stock villains. There was also a rich activity associated with the trading of comic books. Usually a weekend activity, it involved one party coming to the other party's home with a stack of comics and then an effort to see if two *Donald Ducks* were equivalent in trade to one *Superman,* etc. It occupied hours and involved the evolution of the bundling of deals of various shapes. It was fun and perhaps instructive for future financial wizards. For me, just fun. There was also a large number of motion pictures, both A films and B (see below) which found their *raison d'etre* in the war. In addition, the action serials, so prominent in the Saturday children's programs, also went to war even as the regular cartoon features saw *Bugs Bunny* and others take on the Japanese and the Nazis.

Movies, of course, as well as radio formed the major source of entertainment during those years. Movies required some effort, since one had to get to a theatre to see the film. Radio was the cheaper and more comfortable option, since it required no financial contribution after the radio itself was purchased and could be enjoyed at home and in casual dress. (It was an era in which adults did not go to movies or travel in "casual" clothing.) In even minor metropolitan areas, movie theatres ran two different programs (one A picture and one B picture) each week. On Saturday mornings, boys and girls (at my age always separate) were admitted for about ten cents for a several hour festival of films, cartoons and serials. Early Saturday mornings were often characterized by a near frantic search for returnable bottles. A quart beer bottle had a returnable deposit of 5 cents and a small beer bottle or *Coke* or *Pepsi* bottle was redeemable for two cents. If you could get your hands on two quart bottles and maybe three small bottles, you had the price of admission plus a candy bar or a box of *Milk Duds* or *Good & Plentys*. For your admission, you got literally hours of entertainment. Usually you could count on an action serial, a newsreel, several cartoons and then two films. It was possible that both might be Bs but not always. Hollywood studios in the so-called "Golden Age" produced A films (feature films) which had relatively large budgets, good scenic design, reasonable plots, realistic sets and major stars, as well as a competent cast of believable character actors. Bs were usually low budget, weakly scripted, had few recognizable stars and relied heavily on the use of stock footage. They were often *schlock* or nearly so. The studio system, as it then existed, had many monopolistic or near monopolistic features, one of which involved theatres renting A and B films. Later broken up by a U.S. Supreme Court decision; in the '30s and '40s, if a theatre wished to show a studio's A pictures, it was required to rent the B films as well. This was really the origin of the famous "Double Feature" of that day. Adults (we would have said "grown-ups") were at least guaranteed one A film on a double bill – though they were not guaranteed that it would be a good film. So children flocked to Saturday morning matinees and parents were provided with three or four child free hours. In my 80s,, it seems clear to me that both parties felt themselves rewarded and enriched.

Radio was free and offered significant varieties of entertainment, though it did require more imagination. It effectively programmed for the entire family. In the late morning and early afternoon, programs were geared to the women's market and featured some forms of early game shows, but, primarily, serial tales of the tribulation of middle class womanhood in various forms of social, economic and domestic peril. These were the famed "Soap Operas" – so-called because they were often sponsored by soap manufacturers and were intensely dramatic. Among the titles were *Our Gal Sunday* and *Portia Faces Life*. As the afternoon waned, and children came home from school, the afternoon programs were primarily serial adventures aimed at children. These adventures, whether *Captain Midnight* or western adventures, all required the exercise of individual imagination – each child had to create his or her own sense of the scenes, the moods and the characters without any visual clues.

Music, of course, as in the movies, provided useful hints, as did "sound effects" (two coconut shells in sand sounded like horses' hoofs and a tin sheet vigorously plied stood in for thunder), but the final product for each child was produced "between his ears," in the phrase of the day. This phenomenon was probably most fully illustrated in a program which, I think, aired on Saturday morning. It was called *Let's Pretend*. As I recall, the drama was often a fairly elaborate fantasy, but, of course, the colors, shapes and sizes – the mental visualization of all elements – was provided by the imaginative faculties of the radio audience. As late afternoon programming waned, stations *segued* into the evening news, which I remember was primarily national. Most parents had their favorite national commentator, such as Gabriel Heatter or H. V. Kaltenborn.

Allowing for dinner, which virtually all families ate together without electronic accompaniment, evening programs began about 7:30 p.m. High on everyone's list of favorites was *The Lone Ranger,* which, I think, was on three nights a week. It is probably best described as transitional programming, as the bedtimes of children signaled a movement into what we would now call "prime time." For a small child, with an appropriate bedtime, little was known about "adult programming." Indeed our modern usage provides a startlingly different meaning for the term than was then the norm. On weekends, greater latitude was possible, and we were well aware of programs like *Gangbusters*. That program began with a staccato burst of machine gun fire, cars roaring, sirens blaring – so loud and so demanding of attention that for half a century or more after, people would use the expression that an overly exuberant thing, or person, "came on like Gangbusters!" Sunday afternoons, still characterized by large, sometimes extended, family dinners, offered little on the radio that was of interest to children. There were then few NFL football broadcasts or other major sports regularly available. There was opera, though it was listened to in a limited number of homes, and there were other "uplifting" programs. I suspect, however, that most middle class families, such as my grandmother's, listened to *One Man's Family*. It was, to me, totally soporific – a completely banal, ongoing soap opera following the vicissitudes of "one man's family" in excruciating and monotonous detail. Usually, my father napped during this period while his sisters and my mother cleaned up after Sunday dinner. There was little then which would indicate that an era of *gender norming* was someday to come.

By way of contrast, Sunday evening was a delight. It was comedy night. In our family it began with Fred Allen, a witty and imaginative monologist joined by a cast of characters who inhabited a fictional neighborhood known as *Allen's Alley*. Fred would journey through the alley each week chatting with one or more characters such as the stereotypical Southerner, Senator Claghorn. Allen was followed by the *Jack Benny* show. Benny was something of a comic genius who worked well with various foils: his announcer, Don Wilson; his bandleader, Phil Harris and, in the parlance of the day, his boy singer, Dennis Day. Once again, imagination was necessary to populate and understand these universes. However, imagination, music and very effective use of sound effects created comic communities which all could enjoy. Certainly, both programs were diverting and very funny and were intelligible to two or more generations. Amazing to relate in the second decade of the 21st century, with the exception of an occasional and often very funny *double entendre*, they managed week after week to amuse without constant references to genitalia. Both programs, as well as others, such as Edgar Bergen and Charlie McCarthy, made use of well-known guest stars on occasion. Sometime between 8:00 and 9:00 or 9:30 p.m., depending upon my current age, bedtime arrived. Always resisted, it, nevertheless, had its hidden attractions. We still lived in a world whose rhythms had been established long before my birth. So, Monday was still washday and Saturday was still bath night, and so on. When one bath a week was the norm, the development of floating soaps, such as *Ivory,* and *Swan* and so on represented a cost saving because one did not have to search for the soap under the surface of water made opaque by a week's worth of grime. For some reason, one of my great joys, almost sensuous and sybaritic, was to bathe, put on clean pajamas and carefully slide in between the freshly cleaned sheets of a very tightly made bed. Not opening the covers, but sliding under them into a snugly fitting compartment of sorts. There I would rest content and sleep very well – though, like most small boys, I rarely slept badly. Why this rather elaborate ritual pleased me so much I cannot say and should any analyst wish to offer explanations, I suggest that at my current age they probably would have little value. Another cherished memory of childhood, remembered by many, was the joy of "tricking" one's parents and reading under the covers by flashlight after being put to bed.

Then, as now, we were awash in a sea of advertising – though the water was probably somewhat shallower. I am rather sure that there was less broadcast time allotted to advertising in those days, but certainly ads were omnipresent on the radio, as well as in print. One of the Sunday night shows, Benny for a while I think, was sponsored by the American Tobacco Company's *Lucky Strike* cigarettes. Just as the war began, the *Lucky* cigarette pack turned from green to white and for a time they used the slogan, "*Lucky Strike* green has gone to war." Later in the war, they would begin their radio ads with a dramatic outburst of Morse Code (the letters LSMFT) followed by the message, "L S M F T: *Lucky Strike* Means Fine Tobacco"— playing off the use of Morse Code in military communications, which had been made familiar by the war. In print, doctors and movie stars, including Ronald Reagan, touted one or another brand of cigarettes as better, smoother, etc. Everyone was prepared to "Walk a mile for a Camel." *Old Gold* cigarettes, usually with a doctor's photo, pointed out that with *Old Golds*, you could be sure there was not "a cough in a carload." Besides cigarettes, there was *Jello* and *Jergens Lotion* and various types of over-the-counter vitamins and medications. By modern standards, there was a dearth of automobile advertising since new cars for the civilian market were not manufactured between 1942 and 1944/45. Production capacity in the automotive industry was devoted exclusively to military production. Auto companies, and other manufacturers of civilian goods, which were restricted by governmental regulation from civilian production, did, at least occasionally, produce ads which were primarily designed to keep the brand name before the public.

There was one other form of entertainment, less demanding of imagination, but still delightful. When Sunday arrived, the local newspaper provided what seemed an enormous number of comic strips. They ran the gamut from relatively crudely drawn strips such as *Maggie and Jiggs*, which chronicled/satirized the Irish *nouveau riche* or the *Katzenjammer Kids*, whose interest was in the German immigrant caricature, through the rural *Barney Google*, to adventure strips like *Smiling Jack* and the really well drawn, often meticulous, *Prince Valiant,* set in a time period somewhere near the start of the second millennium A.D. The artwork perhaps culminated in the superbly drawn *Terry and the Pirates. Terry and the Pirates* had been an adventure strip set in Asia, and as such had nibbled around the edges of the Japanese adventure in China, but after the U.S. entered the war, the strip went to war. Its creator, Milton Caniff, also began another strip, *Steve Canyon*, which focused directly on World War II. The influence of the latter two was well demonstrated when Madame Chiang Kai-shek (the wife of Generalissimo Chiang Kai-shek, the leader of the Chinese government during the war) came to be identified with a character from *Terry and the Pirates*, the quite sultry figure known as the "Dragon

Lady." Another example, drawn from *Steve Canyon,* was the appearance in the strip of Army Air Force Colonel "Flip" Corkin, who was much more than loosely based on the real life hero Colonel Philip Corcoran. Corcoran directed U. S. Army Air Force logistical and other support in the China-Burma-India Theater for British General Orde Wingate and his *Chindits* – long range penetration groups who fought behind Japanese lines. Similar support was also provided for the American troops under the command of General Frank Merrill (*Merrill's Marauders*). In passing, it should probably be noted that, for economic reasons, only the Sunday papers had their comic strips in color. Weekday cartoons, were in black and white – as was most of our reading and viewing world. The use of color in movies (Technicolor) was also expensive and, therefore, relatively rare. Disney films were in color, as were films such as *The Wizard of Oz* and *Robin Hood,* but by far the largest number of films, even A films, were in black and white.

It was a wonderful treat, after Mass on Sunday, to sit down to a feast of funnies, along with breakfast and a cup of coffee. My mother and father were both as serious about their intake of caffeine as they were their intake of nicotine. My mother prepared my coffee with great care. I would now estimate that it ran 90 or 95% milk or cream to perhaps 5% coffee. But, diluted or not and well sugared, it too was a Sunday treat. It also illustrates another point." Coffee" or no "coffee," much of our entertainment and by far the majority of our intellectual stimulation necessarily involved reading, with or without the use of imagination – usually with. In that era reading was the basis of all of our education and virtually all of our knowledge of the world. It was, as for many to a large degree it still is, also the principal source of relaxation and humor. In the more parochial world of my boyhood, on Dec. 7, 1941, most Americans had to find out where Pearl Harbor was! That knowledge, and much more that grown-ups and children would soon want to know was likely to come from newspapers. Radio and movies (all film showings were normally preceded by "newsreels" – five or ten minutes of film of air raids, the fires of the London Blitz and similar dramatic events) played a useful but clearly subsidiary role. It was radio which alerted us to the raid on Pearl Harbor, but the newspapers that told us where it was, what it was and why it was important. Newspapers fleshed out headlines for us. In the 1940s most small or medium sized cities had at least two daily newspapers, one morning and one evening. Larger cities might have a half-dozen or more. Newspapers were the stars of World War II's information world. No matter what the financial exigencies we faced, the Kellys never were without newspapers. Reading also provided readers with broader and subtler knowledge. Magazines, such as *Colliers, The Saturday Evening Post, Harper's* and *Atlantic* introduced their readers to political and military leaders, to concepts of strategic thinking and to the ideas underlying institutions such as conscription and rationing. *Life* and *Look* provided a plethora of pictures to fill the mind with illustrations of production lines, troops training, parachutists and planes and tanks and guns. Each enabled Americans to form a more accurate picture of the war which was so all encompassing.

If that world was, overall, slower, some means of communications, which still involved reading, were perhaps faster than they are today. I have, apparently, always had an affinity for the postal service. My mother delighted in telling a tale of me, at perhaps two, in a playpen on the front porch, having shed all of my clothes, cheerfully shouting out, "Hello my friend the mailman!" when that figure arrived. The letter carrier was ubiquitous at that time. A first class stamp cost 3 cents, until 1950 or so, an air mail stamp, 6 cents. A post card, truthfully, was described as "the penny post." Air mail letters posted in Los Angeles on Monday would arrive in Chicago or Cleveland on Tuesday. Residential customers got two deliveries each day, businesses got three of four. People regularly communicated by post of one sort or another, and personal mail was the norm. So important was the mail that, for morale purposes, as we sent millions of men overseas, a special post, *V-Mail,* was instituted to maximize the use of cargo ships. Letters to and from GIs overseas, were microfilmed to save weight and space in shipping and handling and then dispatched.

A more clipped form of reading was still necessary to deal with telegrams. Western Union had long since essentially replaced the telegraph with the teletype machine but it still prided itself on the rapidity of its service. The usual personal telegram was restricted (for reasons of economy) to ten words or less and conveyed ideas rather tersely as a result. During the war, the arrival of a Western Union telegraph messenger in a neighborhood was usually viewed with alarm. In most front windows, there would be a red-bordered rectangular flag with one or more blue stars on a white field. Each star represented a son or husband in the armed forces. The great fear was a telegram which would begin "The Secretary of War (or Navy) regrets to inform you that ...." The rest would be a notification of (WIA) wounding, being taken prisoner or being killed in action (KIA). The latter, the most feared, would turn the blue star to gold.

The most private and intimate form of communication available was the telephone. In an era when many seven year olds have their own cell phones, it seems strange to stipulate that during World War II the telephone, was, as yet, nowhere nearly universal. Indeed, the coming of the Great Depression and its economic imperatives had seen an absolute decline in the number of private phones in use. Not until after the war would the number of family phones return to the number in use in 1929. There were times when our family did not have a phone. Phone numbers were then only five digits, with no prefixes necessary. My grandmother's number in Syracuse was 58290. Long distance calls were quite expensive, ranging up to $1.00 per minute. On the other hand, local calls were only five cents and public telephones, phone booths, were virtually everywhere. It goes without saying what a debt Superman owed to the telephone company ("Ma Bell" – a virtual monopoly) and its booths, for all those quick changes through which Clark Kent became Superman. Though even as a boy, I sometimes wondered how, or if, he was able to recover all those blue suits. Comedians too were indebted to the phone company for any number of comedic bits, most of which involved the "party line." A party line was a single circuit which served multiple families. It was most common in rural and other underserved areas. Family A on the line might have a ring of three short rings; Family B, two longs and a short; Family C, a short followed by a long and then another short. If you wanted to make an outgoing call and you picked up the receiver and the phone was in use, etiquette required you to wait until the line was free. Most of the humor was derived from eavesdropping (a real no-no), from seemingly interminable waits for the line to come free and from various violations of etiquette. My only direct experience with the party line came when we were at my Aunt Lilly's house in Saranac Lake. Cities because of population size had economies of scale which enabled them to dispense with party lines long before more rural areas.

CHAPTER 3
School, Religion and World War II - Continued

As the war continued, so did my progression through the elementary grades. In fourth grade, reunited with Sister Anne Marie, I was happy to reconnect more formally with American History. This was not unique to Cathedral but the normal sequence of the New York State approved curriculum. I suspect that there was an extra emphasis on all things American, due to the war. I think too, that Catholic schools, which were anxious to demonstrate their loyalty to the nation (which had often been challenged in the not so distant past), were even more emphatic in their enthusiasm. It was well within a single lifetime that specious accusations had been circulated about Catholic churches with weapons in their basements anxious to overthrow the Republic and enthrone a pope in Washington. I remember as a small boy on the playground, certainly unaware of the background, talking about guns in church basements.

The war also greatly influenced our knowledge of geography. On December 7, 1941, many Americans had not known where Pearl Harbor was. By December 7, 1942, we knew about Manila and Bataan, about Midway, about Australia and about Guadalcanal. We also knew about Jimmy Doolittle and the Tokyo bombing of April, 1942. Our geographic knowledge was further extended in November, 1942, when the U.S. Army landed in Morocco and Algeria in North Africa. As was true in many families in those days, our family cut out a large map (perhaps one for the European region and another for Asia and the Pacific) from the newspaper and began using small flags or colored pins to show the positions of the Axis enemy and American and/or Allied forces.

In the meantime, life went on. We played "war," but we also played *Hide and Go Seek* and *Red Rover*, and *Kick the Can*. About this time (1943 or so) my family relocated to the small house with no central heating to which I have already referred. The neighborhood, while definitely not upper class, offered some real advantages. It was ethnically Italian, which did not assure a warm welcome for a boy named Kelly. The people next door, however, had around ten children, one of whom was just about my age. There were lots of kids in the neighborhood, which was great. Syracuse averaged about ten feet of snow each winter in those days, and there were two excellent hills for sledding. Of course, even sledding was not always an unalloyed joy. On one occasion, as I, quite happily, was coasting down the hill on my sled, a dog, a Chow, came running out of his yard and bit me on the ankle. Snowsuits and galoshes prevented any real damage but it did put me off dogs for quite a while. The neighborhood in addition to sledding hills also possessed one really excellent vacant lot, large enough for *Red Rover*, although barely passable for sandlot baseball, and baseball was important. It was then truly unchallenged as the "national pastime." College football, while popular, occupied only about eight weekends per year and professional football had only a negligible following. Everybody played baseball – or a derivative such as "stoop ball." When there weren't enough kids for a game, two or three or four boys might get a rubber ball or a tennis ball and play a game of stoop ball. The "batter" would throw the ball against a set of steps. If the rebound was cleanly caught, it was an out. If not, there was an arbitrary set of rules (marginally akin to a "ground rule double" sort of thing), stipulating if the "hit" was a single, double, etc.

Later, when I was in my teens, we had another baseball variant. The batter held a broom-stick and the pitcher delivered a bottle cap. If it was hit, it was in play. It was not without its perils. A well-hit bottle cap was moving at a high rate of speed. If not cleanly caught, as I can testify, it can do substantial damage to one's front teeth. Mostly, we caught them.

If girls are absent here, as indeed they are, it is because most of our games, except *Hide and Seek*, were primarily male. Even in school, on the playground at recess, the boys went one way, the girls another. Perhaps if my sister had lived, and her friends had been in and out of the house, as mine were, there might have been more interaction – though memory suggests that not much was different with my friends who had sisters. I do have one indelible memory of girls at play and that was girls jumping rope. The agility and dexterity displayed by virtually every girl I ever saw jump rope, from the simplest exercise to the complexity of "Double Dutch," always seemed to me to be so well done as to be totally beyond any ability or agility which I then possessed, or ever would.

In school, throughout these years, I was always a full year younger than my classmates and almost always physically the smallest. The age gap, coupled with the fact that my father was only 5'4" tall and my mother barely 5', provides the simplest and most likely explanation for that fact. One result was that I was often subjected to a certain amount of bullying. Sometimes it was merely verbal, which I was able to handle relatively easily, since I was usually able to respond in kind and with good results. I had an extensive vocabulary and a mother who was very fast with a quip and tolerant of a son who was quick to try it on. Sometimes, it involved pushing or shoving in lines in the hall or lunchroom. On the playground at recess, or in the neighborhood, it took more directly physical forms. In those cases, it might involve seizing my cap, or other item which might serve as a trophy, and playing "keep away" with it. This of course would involve two or more tormentors. On still other occasions (though not as many as one might think) more conventional physical confrontations might take place. On the playground, these incidents were limited because it was a relatively small space, and because the nuns kept up direct supervision and refused to countenance too much antisocial behavior. In the neighborhood there were fewer constraints. My mother once said that in the years we lived there, I was paid only one compliment. I had a long and epic fight which raged through several yards and over a fair amount of time with my friend Dick. Finally, fatigue and belated adult intervention brought it to an end. There was no question but that I had lost. On that day, Dick's mother, who had been a spectator, said to my mother, "There was a moment there when I thought he might cry." Of such moments and such incidents are moral victories crafted!

One of the "keep away" incidents with my hat created one of the few things I can remember which momentarily threw my mother off balance. I recovered my hat as always; the game ultimately grew tiresome, but this time there was a bonus. I contracted a case of head lice, presumably from one of the kids who had worn it while I was vainly chasing them. We then wrestled with various lotions and potions and seemingly endless sessions with a "fine-tooth comb," as my mother sought to eliminate not only the lice but the nits (eggs or larvae of lice) from my hair. For my mother, who could brook poverty but associated lice with social degradation, it was a bitter blow. Her "shining boy" had somehow been sullied and she was ashamed. Other than the fine-tooth comb, which hurt, her "shining boy" was oddly indifferent.

In both school and neighborhood, the small boy who hardly ever won a fight did learn that rapid thinking and some planning could easily lend itself to leadership. Not always, but not infrequently, bigger boys could be persuaded to act in ways which smaller boys suggested. It would prove to be a useful life skill. Persuasion can become power. He also learned that a quip or a witty remark could often change the mood of a group and prevent unwanted confrontation.

In addition to buses, Syracuse in the 1940s still had trolley cars. Targeted for extinction in favor of buses, the war, with its rubber shortage, restrictions on automotive production and gasoline rationing, kept the trolleys alive a little longer. In the summer, they were just about totally open. (Safety engineers and insurance executives of today would be catatonic if they had to deal with them.) When the overhead wires sparked, the aroma of ozone filled the air. The seats were upholstered in some kind of straw or wicker, anyway a grass-like mesh material, and I always found the trolleys more interesting to ride. The route to my grandmother's house was a trolley line.

Because we had long since ceased to possess a car, I was early on a seasoned voyager on buses and trolleys, even understanding the often arcane depths of the then omnipresent transfer system. The prevalent public transportation theory of the day was that a single fare should get you anywhere you wanted to go within that transit system. However, if the route past your home did not go directly to your destination, you could reach it by riding to a transfer point. When you boarded the first bus or trolley, you asked for and were given a piece of paper, a transfer. When you reached the end of your line, or a transfer point, you got off the bus or trolley you were on. Then you boarded another line, heading to your destination. As you boarded, you surrendered your transfer to the driver of that vehicle. It could be time-consuming but it was, at least for the young, a learning experience. As fate would have it, I would not own my own automobile until I was twenty-five years old, so these early lessons proved useful to me for a good deal of my life.

An unrelated but wonderful element of my life in Syracuse might be parenthetically mentioned here. In the 1940s, milk was still directly delivered to individual households. Like the trolley, the milk horse had also been given something of a reprieve by the war due to the same considerations, gasoline and rubber. As a result, after I got to know the milkman on our route, I was frequently allowed to ride portions of the route near my house. While not exciting, it was interesting, and the milkman was good company. The horse actually knew the route. After a delivery, the milkman would sort of just flip the reins in the air and the horse would move off, stopping at the next house to be delivered. I suspect that all small boys find the sight of a moving horse actively urinating or defecating quite amusing. I know I did. It was the sort of humor which, like flatulence, has come to replace sophistication in what passes for much of modern entertainment. Our milk company, the *Dairy Lea* milk cooperative, delivered milk in quart bottles, the upper neck of which was bulbous. The cream in the milk rose to fill the neck and was poured off by wives and mothers for coffee and other uses. The neck was sealed by a cardboard cap and a crinkled paper cap. In winter, at temperatures at or below freezing, a column of frozen cream and milk would often push the caps up and rise out of the bottle. It never failed to be remarked upon. Second only to the milk wagon was the ice truck. Many people then still owned what were literally "ice boxes." Precursors of refrigerators, ice boxes were small chests usually lined with metal into which blocks of ice were placed (25 lbs. or so) and which kept food reasonably well. As the ice melted, it dripped, so a chore for larger children was emptying the drip pan. The taste of an ice chip from the wooden floor of the ice truck, with a woody, faintly sweet flavor was a true delight on a summer day.

Neighborhoods were different, more complex, in the 1940s than today. They were alive. There was always movement on the streets, people crossed paths, exchanged a word or a smile or a frown and moved on. Women (most mothers were at home all day, every day) exchanged gossip, or recipes, or stories about their lives or their children. They walked a block or two to the corner store or on some other errand with some social interaction almost sure to occur. When itinerant merchants or tradesmen arrived, they came out to look, to buy, maybe just to congregate, but they came out. In late spring, summer and early fall, the neighborhood had visitors. Among them would be the rag man.

His truck would slowly troll through the area as he called out for rags. Out would come housewives with bags of outgrown or worn out clothing and underwear to see what price might be obtained. Next might appear the vegetable truck. It was often an uncomfortable distance to a large grocery store for fresh produce. Again, a truck would appear, slowly moving through the neighborhood vending fruit and vegetables. Again, a number of potential customers would emerge from their homes and then sales, or at least some dickering would begin. Among the children, the favorite good weather merchant traveler was always the knife sharpener. He was always on foot, with his sharpening wheel strapped on his back.

I have no way of knowing what the weight was but it certainly appeared to be punishing. There was a large, granite grinding wheel, fixed to a wooden frame, with a grinding apparatus attached. I assume it had to weigh fifty pounds or more. He was a welcome sight and was usually greeted by a significant number of women, with a number of knives and scissors offered for sharpening by each. As he honed each knife, the contact between steel and stone sent up a high pitched shriek and sparks frequently flew. I don't know how far he walked each day or whether he had a car nearby with which to wend his way home from the day's work but I do know those stops, which probably were 30 to 45 minutes, each formed high points for the neighborhood when they occurred. Each visit set off a series of social (and perhaps economic) actions which relieved boredom.

As I moved from fourth through sixth grade, I was exposed to Ancient (Classical) History and the medieval world. In English we read widely and began to parse and to diagram sentences. Somewhere around sixth or seventh grade we were introduced to a series of books on English and American literature published by the L. W. Singer Company. These were all entitled, *Prose and Poetry* with a specific addendum for each book. Thus, "*Prose and Poetry for Enjoyment, For Appreciation, Of America, Adventures, Of England*" and so on. Each book contained an interesting blend of short stories, plays and poetry. They ranged, in *Adventures* for example, from *The Midnight Ride of Paul Revere* to *Casey at the Bat*, and from Edward Lear to Emily Dickinson. Each also contained a remedial reading section. Each poem or story also contained a glossary of words designed to improve vocabulary and to correct pronunciation. I still think it was the best set of texts for the teaching of English that I have ever seen.

Once again, in this period of my life, there was to be an age-related religious problem. This time it involved the sacrament of Confirmation. The appropriate age was twelve; I was eleven. Consultations were held, words were spoken and it was decided that it was wisest for me to proceed with my class. Confirmation, we were told, indicated our maturation in matters of religious faith. As a Jewish boy at his *bar mitzvah* says, "Today I am a man" so, we were instructed, we were moving into adulthood. We should be prepared, if necessary, to suffer for the faith. A specific example was provided for us. During one of the Roman persecutions, a young boy, an acolyte named Tarcisius, was charged with the task of taking the Holy Eucharist (Holy Communion) to imprisoned Christians facing martyrdom. *En route,* he was detected and beaten to death. He then came to be revered as a martyr and an exemplar. As a symbol of our new status, the bishop, who conferred the sacrament, would lightly strike each child as he administered the blessing. (And full many an exaggerated tale of heavy handed bishops knocking children to the ground gained considerable credence as the day approached. I am happy to report that there were no fatalities.)

Tarcisius was also the patron saint of altar boys and I had, in an extremely limited way, followed in his path. The cathedral in Syracuse was named St. Mary's. That was also, indeed, the formal name of the Cathedral school. The Roman Catholic Bishop of Syracuse then was the Very Reverend Walter Foery. On solemn occasions, when the Bishop celebrated High Mass, his entry into the church was preceded by a group of acolytes, candle bearers – I think we were six in number, three on each side of the aisle. As acolytes, we literally carried the light. Each boy (there were as yet no females allowed on the altar during Mass, other than a bride at her wedding) carried a candle atop a long pole, perhaps four feet long. This was the ritual of the Latin Mass of the pre-Vatican II Roman Catholic Church, so we were dressed almost as miniature priests. We wore a full black cassock (endless buttons) with a surplice, a sort of full white linen blouse, and a very heavily starched Eton collar with a flowing black bow at the neck. It is possible that on the most solemn of occasions, Christmas and Easter, we wore red cassocks.

I was very young when I enlisted, or was conscripted by sister, as an acolyte. Many of the services at which we appeared were very long. On an early occasion, I think Midnight Mass at Christmas, the ritual called for a litany. A litany is a series of prayers consisting of an invocation followed by a response, e.g., "St. Peter" – "Pray for us" (in Latin, "ora pro nobis"). It was of course all in Latin at that time. Acolytes were supposed to sit, stand, or kneel as required but to be fully silent. I found myself in some danger of falling asleep, and, in an effort to stay awake, I said the responses aloud.

During that time, virtually all altar boys were trained by nuns. They took the responsibility very seriously. When school started after Christmas, Sister took me to task for "talking on the altar." I pleaded my case for extreme fatigue and added the additional mitigating circumstance that there had been no conversation. My argument had little effect. Well trained altar boys were like a well-trained drill team; they thought and moved as one. And they were **silent.**

The good sisters (and most of them truly were) also supervised the school's corporate visits to Church. There is a Catholic devotion which involves attending Mass and receiving the Eucharist on the First Friday of each month. So, on the first Friday of each month, we would leave school and walk the few blocks to the Cathedral for Mass. All was organized by the nuns, and each sister supervised her own class during the process. When we entered the church and they no longer felt it appropriate to give vocal directions, they switched to crickets. These were small metallic objects which, when pressed, gave off a distinctive, loud click or chirp. One click might mean sit, two stand, etc. During Mass, there was little room for doubt as to which position was to be assumed – the cricket ruled. Years later, when I saw the film, *The Longest Day* and watched the sequence where members of the 82nd Airborne Division were issued crickets as recognition devices for the Normandy jump, I wondered how many of those young men had a flashback to Sister "Mary Benedict," *et al.*; and the rule of the cricket.

I would be remiss in this area if I did not indicate just how fascinating and beautiful the solemn liturgical ceremonies were. The ritual of a solemn high mass, with the chanted incantations, the bells demanding attention to the more solemn moments of the celebration, the dramatic use of incense (what "low church" Anglicans used to call "smells and bells"), formed a virtually choreographed presentation: all "to the greater honor and glory of God." Even agnostics have been known to comment on the pure aesthetic beauty and joy of the event. Acolytes, too, in their own small way were moved by what they saw and happy that they had a role.

Neither new sacraments nor general maturation had armored me against "sin." When I got to the fifth grade, Sister Stanislaus subjected us to seemingly endless repetitions of the exercises which involved the Palmer Penmanship method of cursive writing. We had been exposed to them before, but never in such quantity. The Palmer method required you to write with the motion of your whole arm, not just your fingers and wrist. Properly done, it produces a beautiful and highly legible hand. For some reason I found myself incapable of doing this at all well. I could produce acceptable work, but only if I used just my fingers and wrist. Like many students, before and since, I learned to fake it. I would sit, in mid-class, adeptly moving my full arm in the approved mode while leaving no trace on the paper. The product to be handed in was prepared in a non-approved manner and was well received. These exercises were done in ink, rather than pencil. We were still using pens with metal nibs at the time and the ink had to be replenished by dipping the pen at frequent intervals. This meant that each desk required an inkwell. Accordingly, at the upper right hand corner of each desk, a hole, about an inch and a half or two inches was bored. A glass inkwell of similar dimension was filled with ink and placed in the hole. It served as our source for all exercises done in pen. Useful equipment included a blotter to dry the work before it smeared and a pen wipe (small piece of cloth) to cleanse the nib if the prongs became clogged. If the student who sat in front of you was a girl with rather long pig tails, an awesome temptation arose.

Among the chores which fell to students, either as volunteers or as punishment, was the cleaning of inkwells. I think that only took place once a week. All the inkwells were removed and emptied and the wells were thoroughly rinsed and returned to their places. They also had to be refilled – though that task never fell to me. Another task children were given was clapping erasers. This was a daily exercise, right after school. Erasers were gathered from all the classrooms and brought to the back entrance of the school. A group of boys awaited them and "clapped" them. That is, one eraser was clapped or beaten against another until the chalk dust was expelled. Generations of boys had empirically proven that beating them against the red brick side of the school performed the function far more thoroughly and rapidly than clapping. Generations of nuns had noted that the process left unsightly marks on the wall of the school, which, unless washed, would only be removed by significant amounts of rain. As was usual in these sorts of generational disagreements, the nuns won. I suspect that boys were chosen primarily (or exclusively) for the task on the grounds that the chalk dust would have made unsightly marks on the dark blue jumpers that the girls wore as part of their school uniform. For some reason unknown to me, dark blue trousers, were not regarded in the same light.

Somewhere during these years, another ritual of maturation took place. Now long vanished, it was the arrival of "long pants." In those days, boys, at least "Upstate," wore shorts in the summer and "knickers" or knickerbockers, in the winter. The latter were trouser-like garments which fell only to the knee. They fastened at the knee with buckles, buttons or, if "modern," elastic. A long stocking then covered the leg. I will spare the reader the tales of itchy wool upon the thighs and the often spectacular failure of wartime elastic; it was all part of the territory and no one ever met a boy who was unhappy to get out of knickers and into long pants. The last vestige of this once universal item of male clothing can still be seen upon athletic fields. Football players wear a stylized version each fall; it appears on baseball fields upon the few modern players who allow the stocking colors to show, e.g., Aaron Judge, and, rarely, on the odd golfer who insists on continuing the use of "plus fours." So, somewhere between ages ten and twelve I "got long pants." And very pleased with myself and my parents I was.

While we were at war during virtually all of my time at Cathedral, we were, however, still enfolded in the psychology of the Depression, into which we had all been born and from which all of our parents had suffered hardship. That led to other small jobs that we were required to undertake. For example, school books on top of school tuition were items that our

43

parents paid for, and it was important to keep them in good condition for possible resale. Thus, at the start of every school year, we made book covers. We would come to the kitchen table with our books and a large amount of brown wrapping paper, or grocery bags and we would take the dimensions of the books and make one or more paper templates. We would then cut out of the brown paper a book cover which, when properly folded would enclose the front and back covers and the spine of the book, which would then be protected from rain or stains or whatever. Sometimes, our mothers would make cloth covers for the books, but brown paper was the norm. On the inside front flap we would place our name and address, in case it was ever lost. When I got older, I was amused at my own egotism or self-confidence, because I seemingly always realized that the world revolved around me. My inside address in the early years was always the same. Placed in vertical order I wrote Thomas O'C. Kelly II, —- Elm St, Syracuse, Onondaga County, New York, United States of America, Western Hemisphere, Earth, Solar System, Universe. It might have been a vast and mighty cosmos but I knew where it started.

As the war continued, it increasingly became a center of our life, even for school children. If you went to the movies, you were strongly urged to support the war effort. In school, time was set aside to buy "War Stamps." In an effort to psychologically involve the whole population in the war effort, the government offered low denomination war bonds. For $18.75 you could buy a war bond, do your bit to help, and when it matured, you would redeem it for a $25.00. Few lower class people and fewer children were able to pony up that much money all at once, so various schemes, including payroll withholding, were offered. For children, the offer was war stamps. Each school child had a war stamp book, modeled on the department store merchandise stamp books then popular with many families. Fill a book of stamps and then redeem it for merchandise. In school, during the weekly war stamp period, a child could buy one or more war stamps for ten cents each. When you had purchased 187 stamps, you turned in your stamp book, plus five cents ($18.75) and you were awarded a $25.00 war bond. Competition among children and classes was encouraged. High achieving children were awarded gold or silver stars.

In addition to war bond drives, children also came to the fore in the collection of scrap metal, and other items theoretically to be turned into weapons of war. During one memorable summer, the goal was the collection of milk weed pods. We were told that *kapok*, essential to the making of life jackets, was scarce because Japanese conquests in the Pacific had effectively removed access to it. As a result, we scattered across weed-infested areas, the fringes of forests and swamps in search of milkweed pods. I don't think I ever heard how successful the program was – or even if it mattered. These things arose, were publicized, were attacked and then, as a rule, never heard of again. Still another project was the collection of tinfoil. In those days, items like chewing gum and cigarettes came wrapped in tinfoil. What it represented I no longer remember, but collecting it was a zealous pursuit. I spent a great deal of time peeling the tinfoil off the inner packaging of cigarettes (and chewing gum) and rolling it into balls to be turned in. I believe I did a disproportionally large amount because both of my parents were very heavy smokers, so I had access to an unusual amount of raw material. In a dissimilar context, I had what I think was the family's only experience with the "Black Market" during the war. The black market was the illicit sale (outside the required rationing program) of rationed goods. My father took me with him, probably on a Sunday, to a bar which absolutely fulfilled the definition of "seedy." The purpose of the journey was to purchase several cartons of cigarettes "off the books." He was successful.

Cigarettes were among the heretofore "normal" consumer goods which were suddenly in short supply due to the war. The scarcity was ostensibly due to the demands of the armed forces. Few will now remember that cigarettes were so much a part of life in those days that small packages of them were included in the field rations provided to the troops. Smoking two or three packs a day, my mother and father were often hard-pressed to find enough "coffin nails" (a common usage of the period) and ended up smoking some very odd brands, e.g., *Wings*, when their favorites, *Pall*

Malls, were unavailable. In the then prevailing climate, it was not unusual for me at six or seven to be sent to the store to pick up a pack or two of cigarettes. No one ever thought to refuse to sell them to me, nor did I ever think to smoke them. Not only did my parents, at least occasionally, send me out to purchase cigarettes, they also found it useful to have me manufacture cigarettes for them. In those days, virtually all drug stores and sundry stores sold loose tobacco and "cigarette papers." Old cowboy movies often had one or more characters "rolling their own" as they delivered expository dialogue. Loose tobacco was not subject to the strict rules of pre-packaged "butts." Enterprising individuals soon provided a small machine, perhaps 9" x 3 or 4", with a sort of belt which formed a pouch. Loose tobacco was poured into the pouch, a cigarette paper was inserted and the handle pulled from one end to the other, producing a cigarette. As children proved to be useful in the coloring of margarine (see below), so they were useful in making cigarettes.

Even time both natural and industrial was differently constructed during the war. Most men, and later women industrial workers, still worked a five-and-a-half or six day week despite the efforts of unions to establish the five day, forty hour week as the new, progressive norm. The war saw not only the continuance of a forty-four or forty-eight hour week, but many workers seeking and receiving extensive amounts of overtime hours. Overtime hours were normally compensated at one and a half or two times the normal rate of pay. That is, if normal hourly pay was $1.00 per hour, the overtime worker got $1.50 or $2.00 for each overtime hour. The same labor scarcity that brought women into war work also made overtime a part of the war effort. (In passing I would note that in 1943, the U.S. minimum wage was thirty cents an hour and the average annual wage, about $2,000.) Those years also saw more daylight. The federal government mandated year round Daylight Savings Time or "War Time" as it was called. Instead of setting the clocks forward, as is the norm for summer Daylight Savings Time, clocks were set ahead, not seasonally, but for the duration of the war. Presumably, the extra daylight hours, focused on the workday, would increase industrial productivity.

During each year of the war, additional items of food, clothing and light industrial products were determined to be essential to the war effort and either added to the list of products to be rationed or otherwise restricted. I can remember accompanying my mother on a visit to the local branch of the Office of Price Administration ration board in Syracuse as she sought to obtain additional coupons for shoes for me. She thought I would be bored, so she left me outside to amuse myself while she went in to conduct her business. Looking around, I noticed group of men, digging a trench. I idly wandered over. It must have been around lunchtime because they all downed tools, unwrapped sandwiches and sat down on the edge of the trench to eat. Presented with a view of their backs, I suddenly realized that each man had the letters POW stenciled on the back of his blue denim jacket. It was startling and, indeed, a bit frightening to realize that I was in close proximity to six or so veterans of Hitler's armies. I decided, quite needlessly I am sure, that the other side of the building needed my attention. My mother, parenthetically, did get the coupons, and I got new shoes.

Apropos new shoes, there was then available a new and wondrous device to ensure that children's shoes fit properly. It was a large machine, not unlike a console radio, perhaps four feet high. The child stood on a slightly raised platform with his feet inserted into a sort of slot, with a mark for each foot. The salesman pushed a button and one looked into the aperture and saw an x-ray of the foot inside the shoe. Parents could see how much room there was for the foot to grow before a new pair would be necessary. The wonders of modern science!! I rather doubt that there was much shielding from the radiation and, certainly, no lead apron was provided. How much radiation exposure we had, I guess I shall never know. I do wonder about the salesmen who supervised each visit to the machine. I am told that the use of these machines was banned during the early 1950s. Still, like other perils, we survived that too.

On another level, men and women were confronted with limitations to their wardrobes. Men could no longer have cuffs on their trousers. Women, scandalizing some, found it difficult to get skirts that fell below the knee.

Some men's jackets and most boy's jackets, were styled without lapels, creating a rather unfinished look. Somehow, despite these difficulties, the war years also saw the emergence of the "Zoot Suit." It featured trousers cut wide at the thigh and tapering to perhaps no more than seven inches at the ankle. Wide, heavily padded shoulders characterized the jacket, which was worn several inches longer than a conventional suit jacket. It also featured a wide-brimmed, low-crowned fedora or porkpie hat. It was also known for the use of unusual and vibrant colors. By mid-war they too had fallen afoul of clothing regulations and disappeared. Coffee and tea, like most items which required shipping from overseas, also became difficult to get. Coffee supplies were stretched by the addition of chicory. Tea drinkers, like my mother, who drank both coffee and tea, discovered expedients to stretch supplies. She acquired a metal, inverted bell-shaped, strainer, into which she would put enough loose tea for one cup. When she added boiling water and put it in the cup, it served as a tea bag of sorts. The tea enjoyed, it was set aside to be used again for at least a second, or in dire circumstances, even a third cup. Butter and sugar were also scarce. While butter was rationed, heavy cream apparently was not. I can remember my father, at least starting the butter-making process with an electric beater. I think as it thickened it had to be finished by hand. The government encouraged the use of what was then known as oleomargarine as a butter substitute. Annoyed by this economic assault, the so-called "dairy state" congressional delegation had managed to pass legislation forbidding the adding of food coloring to the product. As a result, oleo, or margarine, came from the store as an unappetizing plastic bag of a white greasy substance. It was, visually, very unattractive. The bag did contain a capsule of coloring material. Small children and other defenseless creatures proved to be quite useful in the incredibly boring and somewhat greasy task of breaking the capsule and then endlessly kneading the package until it became somewhat orange, a color approaching that which might be said to vaguely resemble butter.

Women were particularly bothered by their inability to find attractive, well-fitting stockings which would shape themselves to the leg. Silk and the new miracle fabric, nylon, would do that, but both were reserved for the war effort, nylon e.g., being used in making parachutes. Cotton, lisle and other fabrics simply looked terrible and were, therefore, not wanted. My Aunt Marjorie (my father's sister) who was working for Day Brothers, a large Syracuse department store, found herself engaged on this front. She had charge of a booth to which women brought silk or nylon stockings which had "runs" or "ladders" in them. (A thread in the weave had torn or separated.) Here, the offending stocking was draped over an open, cuplike device and an electric needle vibrated the threads into an apparent whole, erasing the deformation in the weave. She, and her younger sister, my Aunt Joan, also participated in another stopgap measure designed to overcome the loss of shapeliness in the legs of American Womanhood. They, like so many of their suffering sisters, experimented with leg makeup. This substance colored the legs a sort of tan, hoping to make it appear as if stockings were being worn. I thought, but did not say, that it resembled the color of well-kneaded margarine. Since stockings in those days had a seam which ran up the back of the leg, some women went so far as to use an eyebrow pencil in an effort to replicate a stocking seam up the back of the leg.

I saw a good deal of my aunts in those years, usually at my Nan's house. My Aunt Joan, who was a talented pianist, with a Master's degree in music from Syracuse University, decided to teach me to play the piano. I was not a particularly willing or perhaps apt pupil, and Joan's teaching technique leaned heavily on the rhythm of whacking the offending hand with a ruler until it understood what it was to do. Margie was a quite gifted soprano who facially and physically greatly resembled Lily Pons, a noted opera singer of the era. Margie frequently gave recitals, with Joan as her accompanist. On a few occasions, I was in attendance – though why they were saddled with a small boy, I do not know. I found the occasion and music interesting, as were the refreshments on occasion. The exclusively adult conversation which followed was quite dull.

Not unlike modern grandparents with new electronic devices, my grandmother found the complexities of rationing somewhat baffling. Every person had a basic ration, represented by a book of stamps. Red stamps were for meat products, blue for sugar, vegetables, etc. If you bought two pounds of meat and it "cost" less than the full value of your ration stamp, you were entitled to "change." Change was represented by "tokens" worth one or more points. Nan was never fully comfortable with the system and, whenever possible, as she headed out to do her weekly marketing, she would borrow me to accompany her. I would attend her, answer questions and ensure that she got her ration's worth and whatever "change" was appropriate.

My mother had a butcher, Mr. Drescher, who had provided meats for us since before the war. (Many, perhaps most, families then patronized a butcher shop – that is, they did not get their meat from a supermarket.) When meat rationing was introduced, the government's rule was "first come, first served." That is, there were to be no favors; what was available went to whoever first appeared before the counter. In point of fact, most independent butchers, were prepared to take care of their regular customers first. Beneath almost every counter, there were pre-wrapped packages of the more desirable cuts of meat awaiting the arrival of the store's "regular" customers. Years later, talking about Syracuse with my father-in-law, George Schiller, who had grown up in and around Syracuse prior to World War I, I was to discover that Mrs. Drescher, was his sister, Clara. It was one of those "small world moments" which underline our lives.

At home life proceeded. My mother's condition varied from time to time but never improved. Occasionally there would be hospitalizations and she would return: with shorn hair, new scar and hope as her regular companions. My father and I were often in disagreement, and the fact that he was still bigger and stronger than I usually led to abrupt and sometimes painful endings to our differences. When we were engaged in this form of activity, my mother's voice would often be heard, calling out, "Not in the head, Tom, don't hit him in the head." It was often efficacious. There were, however, warm and amusing moments, and while the life I lived was sometimes unpleasant, it was hardly Dickensian. My *contretemps* with my father were not I think unusual for the day and time. About this time (c. 1943/4) we moved to the house I have mentioned, which lacked central heating. I was given the bedroom which adjoined the kitchen and the coal stove, which was the source of heat. My parents decided that the room was too dark and needed to be brightened; so they decided to put up new wallpaper. They chose a paper which consisted primarily of light colors, in vertical stripes. I should note here that neither of them had ever papered anything before. After they had finished, including valiant efforts to get and keep all the vertical stripes vertical, and aligned, it took me no more than two or three days to overcome the slight tinge of vertigo I experienced on first entering the room. (No.; Given the state of our domestic economy, there was no way to start over.) But, it was a family thing and, after my father got over being furious, we all found it funny. In the cold weather, as I fell asleep, my last sight was the plates on the stove glowing red, as my father stoked and banked the stove for the night.

It was there, too, during one Lent, that my father gave up alcohol as a Lenten penance. (Giving something up for Lent, as, for example, candy for a child, was a rather common Roman Catholic practice of the period.) During those six weeks, I came to understand how he had been able to enchant my mother when they were courting. He was charming, highly articulate, caring and considerate. He was quite interesting to talk to, and talk we all did as we played board games, such as *Parcheesi* and *Monopoly*. He was almost a different man entirely. However, Lent, like all things, came to an end, as did his abstinence.

Unbeknown to me at the time, a number of changes were in the offing, and our years in Syracuse were drawing to an end.

CHAPTER 4
Syracuse to Buffalo; Cathedral to Timon – 1947-1952

Sometimes ideas and events collide and change results. During the years 1946-48 what had been the common elements of my life's experience began to change. In 1946, I moved upstairs at Cathedral and entered seventh grade. The nun who presided was called Sister Victoria. Ours was to be a strained relationship. She might well have served as a prototype for all the "mean" or "mad" nun stories which often seem to dominate reminiscences of life in Catholic schools. She disliked "only" children, and particularly disliked boys who were only children. There were only two of us, a friend called Mike Peal and me. If she was on the warpath, she would come down the aisle to your desk, grab a handful of hair and attempt to pull you straight up, out of your desk. In those desks, which were screwed tightly to the floor, you could not come straight up. It was necessary to slide out to one side or the other, and then stand up. I was able to circumvent this tactic, once I had experienced it, by getting, and keeping, a crew cut.

Few parents at that time were prepared to defend children who complained about their teachers, whether in public or parochial school. Usually, such a complaint simply resulted in another punishment administered at home, together with an admonishment not to annoy your teacher. A modern teacher might not be blamed for envying the circumstance. Aware of that possibility, I complained only softly and tactfully until Sister Victoria over-played her hand. Her attitude became overt in relation to my report card. It was probably in October or November that I was given a grade of 80 or so in silent reading. I had never had a grade below 95 in silent reading. My mother was instantly attentive. A meeting was arranged, and when Sister proved to be adamant, I was, quite suddenly, withdrawn from Cathedral Academy.

I was enrolled in another Catholic school which was marginally closer to my home and, academically, life went on. Other events were, however, pending. My mother's father had been a successful building contractor in New York City, primarily in the Bronx, until his death in 1918. His brother had continued the firm after his death. Nearly thirty years later, one property still remained in the estate. In late 1946 or early 1947, that property was sold and the proceeds distributed. My father was always prepared to believe that the grass had to be greener somewhere else. The unexpected windfall seemed to fulfill the hope that permeated the household, that someday, somehow, their "ship would come in." With the money from the Kane es-tate available, his optimism came to focus on Buffalo. He had grown up there and he knew that a good many of his father's friends were still there, and he thought he might avail himself of their good offices. So too might his boyhood friends prove helpful. In any event, after discussion and delay, it was decided that the Kellys would "Shuffle off to Buffalo."

In the fall of 1947, we found ourselves in Lackawanna, New York, just outside South Buffalo and in residence in the Hotel Erie, not coincidentally owned by a boyhood friend of my father's. My father would ultimately find employment as a bookkeeper in one of the steel mills. I was enrolled in Our Lady of Victory Academy (OLVA), which was the parish school for the very imposing Our Lady of Victory basilica. Among my other activities in this period, I would become a tour guide at the Basilica. The church also supervised a fairly large orphanage.

My father set out to cultivate his boyhood friends and the friends of his parents. Little seemed to result from this activity, though he was assid-uous in its pursuit. I did meet a few interesting people in this early period.

One of my father's old classmates, who had inherited his father's business as a funeral director, was of particular interest to me. He still lived in the old mansion/funeral parlor. Behind the house was an ancient barn which had been the stable for the horses that drew the hearse. I remember little of the man or his children, whom I knew only briefly, but I did enjoy the barn and, to a lesser degree, the house where I gave my imagination free rein. The ensuing mental pictures ranged from "The Addams Family" to "Nightmare on Elm Street." In retrospect, nothing of significance, economically or socially, resulted from the move, though the change of schools, first in Syracuse, and then to Buffalo left me without much of a social network. My mother spoke little of the move (and less of the money) other than to hope that my father's "plans" would materialize. She was busy reconstructing links with physicians who might be of assistance to her, though by this time, I think she had little hope for anything other than palliative care. Patience was her watchword. She even taught me a mildly amusing verse about it (and men and women):

> Patience is a virtue
> Find it where you can
> It's seldom in a woman
> And never in a man.

Phenobarbital was her constant prescription. I understood it to be a reasonably effective agent in preventing or limiting seizures. She also had other medications for the alleviation of pain. I was spending a great deal of time with her after school each day, at least until my father got home from work. I guess I was some sort of combination of son, sounding board, *confidante* and early warning system, though there were few dramatic episodes in this period. She frequently told me stories of her growing up, her interactions with her sisters, tales of the nuns at Holy Angels (Fort Lee, New Jersey) and the years before she and my father married. She was about eight years old when her father died, and all the girls, with the exception of the oldest sister, Kitty, went to Holy Angels. It was a boarding school, not an orphanage, and I assume her Uncle Patsy, her father's brother and partner, had made some sort of special arrangement. Monica, the youngest sister, was probably less than two when they arrived. There was no sense of strain in any of this. My mother was an excellent *raconteur,* and at the time, as I have indicated, I had an extremely limited social circle. Living in a hotel also meant that there were only limited opportunities for outdoor activities. I did, very briefly, manage a paper route while we were in Lackawanna, but once again we were traveling. In June of 1948, I graduated from eighth grade and my mother and I left for Saranac Lake where we were to spend the summer with my father's sister, Lilly, and her family. Saranac Lake was famous as the place where Dr. Trudeau had gone, in the 19th Century to "cure" his tubercular osis, and the clear air in the mountains had done just that. The result was that from the 1870s onward tubercular patients had flocked to Saranac for the cure. Even Robert Louis Stevenson had come in the late 1880s – though personally he hated both Saranac and his time there. "Cure cottages," where patients spent hours on the porches breathing the clean mountain air, sprang up throughout the village, and it seemed as if half the mothers were practical nurses. The patients were somewhat cruelly known to the children as "lungers." The Trudeau Institute remains there still.

Over the years, I had spent a good deal of time in Saranac Lake (Franklin County). Less well known than its nearby companion village, Lake Placid, famed as the site of the 1932 (and later the 1980) Winter Olympics. Saranac was only about ten miles away and shared the wonderful scenery and atmosphere of the High Peaks region of New York's Adirondack Mountains. The area was mountainous, liberally sprinkled with lakes, rivers and streams as well as blessed with magnificent forests and secluded valleys. Majestic to behold, it was, summer or winter (we spent a few Christmas vacations there too) a wonderful place for a small boy or early teen. Aunt Lilly and Uncle Jack had five children. My cousin Joe was about a year younger than I and we shared a number of adventures over the years. Perhaps the best of them was our discovery of a very large boulder (almost surely a glacial deposit). It seemed forty or fifty feet tall to me – which probably means it was about fifteen or twenty. The upper surface was nearly flat and wide enough that we could run several steps across it. Once we gained momentum, we would leap off the boulder, grab hold of a sapling and ride it to the ground. Often repeated, the sensation was a splendid mixture of fear and exhilaration and was joy unspoiled. Our mothers, of course, never knew. At nearby Colby Pond, there was another giant rock, this one submerged, that was known to us as "whaleback." Its surface, just beneath the water, was slick, I assume, from algae. We would sit at the top, with our torsos above water, push off and slide to the bottom of the pond. There was also an island with a very high bluff in Middle Saranac Lake. We never dared but the "big kids," presumably high school boys, would jump or dive from the bluff into the water. It wasn't cliff diving at Acapulco, but it certainly thrilled and entertained us.

My Uncle Jack worked for the railroad in Lake Placid where he was the baggage master. He hopped a train to work each morning. My cousin Joe and I would often bring him his lunch. This involved going down to the station in Saranac Lake and taking a late morning train over "to Placid." On occasion, running late, we would, with some pleasure, tinged with admiration for ourselves, hop aboard the moving train. In Placid, we amused ourselves while waiting for the return train. Often this involved trying to get the railroad men to let us operate the turntable. The line to Saranac and Placid was a single track spur line from Lake Clear Junction. If the train was not to back all the way to Lake Clear, the locomotive had to be turned around. A turntable was a section of track, just long enough to hold a locomotive, bridging a pit. The engine was driven onto the turntable (e.g., facing north). The turntable was then rotated and the engine driven off, facing south. It was not a complicated piece of machinery. A single lever activated and stopped it. For boys about twelve years old, operating it and turning a huge steam locomotive was somewhat akin to landing on the moon. We got to do it with some frequency. It was, for me, something of an idyllic summer. The railroad also offered Joe and me another opportunity, this one financial. Lake Placid was a mecca for tourists. Kate Smith, one of the best known entertainers of that era, had a "summer place" in Placid and entertained frequently. Since the town was so small and passenger trains so infrequent, there were few services at the station, and no *red caps*. A red cap was a uniformed railroad employee who carried luggage to and from trains. In those days, all were Negroes. Joe and I thought we would offer our services, so, every Sunday evening (when most visitors left) we would go to Placid and (as we said), "smash bags." There seemed to be no competition – which I never understood, and we almost always would clear two or more dollars each. Since you could get a three-scoop ice cream cone for about a dime, we were plutocrats within our age group – at least in Saranac Lake.

I would occasionally, find a place, on the fringe of a woods or in a meadow, and contemplate the world. I don't think I was on a voyage of discovery or that my thoughts were particularly deep, but I do think I learned a certain amount about being self-aware and self-contained. I probably also, quite unintentionally, was learning something about being able to think and to manage time without outside stimulus. I do assume, however, that most of the time I was just daydreaming. The result was often, but not always, soothing. Once, after such an hour or so, as I headed back to the house, I came across a number of saplings which someone had cut down. I hefted one like a spear and hurled it as far as I could. As it landed, it tore up a patch of ground. With unerring, if accidental, accuracy it interrupted the domestic felicity of a nest of wasps. I made it out of their range at the cost of seven or eight stings. My aunt's training as a practical nurse stood me in good stead and, other than minor discomfort, the incident was without effect.

There were more significant problems. My uncle, who worked for the railroad was, like my father, something more than a social drinker. On occasion, this was disruptive of their domestic tranquility. I also suspect that my mother and I put a real strain on their domestic economy, and probably their felicity too, when my father was late sending funds. I'm also sure that our continued presence was a social and psychological strain on all of them.

I know that there was one period of at least several days, perhaps a bit more, when we were all reduced to eating ketchup or mayonnaise sandwiches. When a check arrived from my father, certainly for no more than perhaps $20.00, the feeling of relief and elation that swept through the house was palpable. Departure for the grocery store was immediate. My mother remained stoic, which she saw, rather proudly, as a Kane trait and was, at least outwardly, cheerful.

The original plan had been for us to return to Buffalo sometime around Labor Day and for me to return to Our Lady of Victory Academy for the ninth grade. My not entirely clear recollection was that all of this was in aid of our transitioning from the Hotel Erie to a flat or apartment of our own, which my father was to have arranged. In any event, something went wrong and after the summer in Saranac, when September came, there was no housing. My mother willy-nilly enrolled me in Saranac Lake High School and, I assume, apologized to Lilly and Jack for the additional imposition. We went on, living in a sort of day to day manner, which was easier for me, I am sure, than it was for her. I had, after all, just turned thirteen and was not very sensitive to atmosphere. I was also among relatives and blissfully unaware that we might be a burden. In addition, surrounded by cousins and responsible adults, I was free. It was not necessary for me to be as completely involved with my mother as was usual. I am now sure that she deeply felt the constraints of living in someone else's house on a sort of indeterminate calendar. Perhaps, even more, her personal inability to alter or ameliorate the situation would have troubled her.

I found public school not to be significantly different from parochial school. The major differences I noted were the absence of a prescribed school uniform, the presence of a school bus to ride and the absence of religion in the curriculum. Offsetting the last, once a week there was early release in the afternoon, for catechism. A bus would take the Catholic kids to the local Catholic Church, where we were provided with "religious instruction." My memories of this are somewhat sparse because it was only two or three months into the school year when Mom and I left Saranac and returned to Buffalo. We had no way of knowing that she then had less than two years to live.

In any event, back at last we went, not to Lackawanna but just a short distance away, into South Buffalo, where my father had grown up. I returned to OLVA to finish the ninth grade. We moved into a second-story flat which I remember as quite pleasant and roomy. We would remain there as long as my mother lived. It was primarily a commercial neighborhood. Directly across the street from the house was a bakery and a small grocery store. Many mornings, as I got up for school, Mom would send me across the street to pick up rolls or some such for breakfast. As I entered the bakery (probably about 6:00 a.m.) the aroma of baked goods and my empty stomach acted as a sort of one/two punch with the sudden flow of gastric juices, caused and intensified by the aromas to almost literally stop me dead in my tracks. The grocery was owned by a Jewish family, whose patriarch spoke a broken English *patois* which verged upon being a stereotype; not unlike that used in a then popular radio and television show called, I think, *The Goldbergs.* He and I got along very well and by late spring or early summer he would often take me with him on his delivery rounds. I enjoyed his company and the deliveries, and I think I grew as a result of his company and our conversations.

Since we were no longer in Lackawanna, my parents decided that I should leave Our Lady of Victory and attend a recently opened, all male high school directed and staffed by priests of the Franciscan Order. Among its other advantages, I was able to walk to school, saving bus fare. So, in September of 1949, I entered Bishop Timon High School, named in honor of the first Roman Catholic Bishop of Buffalo. I studied there (at least occasionally) until I graduated in June of 1952. Before that, I had never before attended a single sex educational institution. I was to find the school stimulating and worthwhile in almost every way. Our class contained about 150 boys. While physically in South Buffalo, Timon was a diocesan high school and, therefore, open to any boy in the diocese. Thus, the classes represented most of Buffalo and its near suburbs, with a logical weight in favor of the southern suburbs. Unknown to me as I entered Timon, I was initiating about a decade in which I would inhabit a predominantly masculine world. Heretofore, all the schools I had ever attended, public and parochial, had included both boys and girls. Now, girls were left behind for my three years at Timon. Similarly, the ensuing three years (1952-1955) in the Army provided highly limited interaction with girls or women and, after the Army, I matriculated at Iona College, like Timon, then an all-male institution (1955-1959).

Overall, the years in Buffalo had a number of interesting and entertaining features. Unknown to my parents, I occasionally found opportunities to find my way to the rail yards and hone my skills in "hopping freights." It remained an exhilarating experience. On a socially more acceptable level, there was a world class botanical garden in South Buffalo, just over the border from Lackawanna. Strangely enough, I always enjoyed roaming through it. I don't think I ever learned anything from it, other than the nearly infinite number of trees and other flora in the world, but I don't think any six months went by without my stopping in for an hour or so.

To use a modern term, when I entered Timon I again experienced what had become "the new normal" for me. I knew virtually no one when school started. I was also entering as a sophomore in a class which had had an opportunity to bond the previous year. I possess no unusual or startling memories, so I can only assume that I had a civil if uneventful start to what would prove to be a highly enjoyable three years at 601 McKinley Parkway. As mentioned, Timon was not a parish or a neighborhood school, but recruited from a much wider geographic region. That probably cut down on pre-existing bonds and cliques and made it easier for me to mix and mingle. The vast majority of the faculty in those days, were priests of the Order of Friars Minor (Franciscans). I was as yet unaware that association with the order would directly influence my life for fifty of the next sixty years of my life. The quality of teaching ranged from superb, through competent to, a single instance of abysmal. My Geometry teacher was young, inexperienced and totally lacking in presence or self-confidence. If you simply stood in the back of the room, you would have assumed you were watching a mime. You would have seen a young instructor with his mouth moving but you, literally, would not have heard a word that was said. He had, I think, surrendered before the end of October. Since math was never my strong point, that was particularly unfortunate for me and I barely eked out a passing grade on the New York State Regents examination. Otherwise, within the curriculum, my *bête noir* was physical education. Still the youngest and mostly the smallest, I was also the "new kid" and, no matter how pleasantly received, afraid of being perceived as younger, weaker, etc. (Rationality in regard to personal presence is not a strong point among fourteen-year-old boys.) I was particularly embarrassed in showering, as less fully physically mature and I was positively humiliated by my sneakers. Until Timon, I had never had formal gym classes. My new classes required sneakers. My father located an affordable pair, which looked rather as if they had been woven out of hay or straw and then heavily lacquered with a tar-like substance. I can still visualize them in all their obscenely shining glory. I ditched gym whenever I could get away with it.

My social studies teachers (then more history than not) were outstanding. I remember, quite fondly, Father Arnold Brown, a young North Carolinian, who struggled to preserve a thin stream of Dixie, without much success among his Yankee Boys. Primarily he discovered that his views on the Civil War lay outside the bounds of orthodoxy for most of us. His sense of humor, however, was never dented or even bruised. At some level, I always thought that the Dixie stuff was put on for effect and may even have served as something of a teaching technique. Certainly, he persuaded me, if not others, that the purpose and meaning of history lay in a search for truth. Father Brian Duffy, a tough, defiantly imperial native of "the City" (he was known, not infrequently, to stipulate that "the best thing that ever came out of Boston was the train for New York"), was a brilliant instructor; perhaps the most effective teacher of English literature that I ever knew. When, for example, we were "doing" Shakespeare, he had us watch Laurence Olivier's film version of *Hamlet*, then quite new, but also listen to the soliloquy on recordings by John Barrymore and John Gielgud. Then we had a classroom discussion of the nature and meaning of the piece. Given the paucity of available media at the time (c. 1950) it seemed almost revolutionary. Whatever else may be said, the Faculty was diligent, intelligent and, for the most part, talented, "… and I learned about teaching from them." Our collective experience with the clerical faculty (the friars) was unusually broad and unusually deep in many ways, as I will illustrate.

In addition to being a talented English teacher, Fr. Brian was also Dean of Discipline for my first two years at Timon. In my senior year, while he continued to teach, he relinquished his disciplinary duties. Shortly after the new academic year began, his loss would be felt. As had been true at Cathedral, at Timon also we faithfully attended mass and communion on the First Friday of each month, though the service was in school. When mass ended, the auditorium was inhabited by more than 600 young men who had, due to the Eucharistic fast, not eaten for about 12 or 13 hours. By tradition, the Senior Class enjoyed the privilege of being the first class to leave the auditorium to go to breakfast. For some reason, no longer remembered, we had displeased the new dean of discipline, who was called Father Damiano. He announced that we would eat after all the other classes. Two classes left for breakfast, leaving the seniors and the freshmen behind. We were seated by homeroom, with the Senior Homeroom classes scattered in different sections of the auditorium. After a time, we began to become restless and one class began to sing "Mammy's little baby loves shortening bread." Fr. Damiano demanded that the singing stop and it did. But as he approached the singing class, other Senior Homerooms took up the song, adding clapping and foot stomping. For perhaps ten minutes, he ran from group to group, which succeeded only in silencing the group he was standing next to. He then left the auditorium as the chorus swelled in victory. After another two or three minutes, the side door to the auditorium opened and Fr. Brian stood on the floor in front of us. He said nothing; he merely stood, pushed up his sleeves and put his hands on his hips. In less than two minutes, you could hear a pin drop. He then spoke. "Gentlemen, kneel down.

We will now say the rosary." And we did. He was the definition of a man who had presence.

Of course, high school was not just about classes and teachers. I did have some sort of extracurricular and social life, albeit somewhat truncated by my mother's illness. My first year at Timon I mostly went to school, came home, maybe stopping for a coke *en route,* and then spent the afternoon with my mother. Depending on the time of year, weather, daylight and such, I might have had some time outdoors after my father came home. My mother, while very ill, "was not an invalid" – she "kept house," as we said in those days, cooked and cleaned and even shopped. My presence was intended as sort of an early warning system should she have a major episode or emergency. In fact, that did not happen, and the time I spent with her was almost always pleasant and frequently instructive. She was quick witted, had a well-developed sense of humor (tending toward the ironic, even sardonic) and was very well read. Looking back, because I spent so much time with her, and because like most teens I was quite self-absorbed, I failed to notice that her condition was deteriorating. I also suspect that she tried to hide her growing frailty from me. The absence of major episodes seemed positive and I failed to notice that she was having to cope with more pain. Neither did I notice that she, always tiny, was physically failing. I don't think that, other than when pregnant, she ever weighed more than 100 pounds.

She still remained the family's voice of sanity. My father was prone to impatience and I, as a teen, was not unwilling to try that patience. I was also prepared to, legalistically "push" the envelope as to just what constituted obedience. When, for example, I was instructed to "do the dishes" after supper, I would have the radio playing near the sink, and I was certainly devoting at least as much attention to the radio as to the dishes. I would, in a leisurely fashion, wash a plate, then rinse the plate, and then dry the plate. My father would begin to mumble and grumble about "efficiency," "energy" and "eternity." I would wash another plate, rinse another plate, etc. My father was now at, "What the hell is the matter with you anyway? I could do that in half the time." My mother would say, "Tom, relax; he's doing it and they will get done." I would wash a plate, rinse, etc. At about that point, my father would erupt, curse at me, in both colorful and blasphemous terms, and then throw me, sometimes literally, out of the kitchen, shouting that he would do it himself. My mother would say, "Tom, that's exactly what he wants you to do." That may have been true. I am not sure how much on my part was conscious behavior and how much was just a combination of ennui, impudence and sloth.

In the summer of 1950, just after the school year had ended, the Korean War broke out. I remember going downstairs, perhaps on my way to the bakery, and seeing the headline announcing the North Korean invasion of South Korea. It was a dull summer for me, most of it spent in the flat. I normally slept late, got up, ate breakfast and then walked over to the library. I would check out four to six books and walk home. I would then talk to my mother and read until my father came home. Most of my reading then tended toward historical novels by authors such as Bruce Lancaster, though I did branch out to science fiction and began a fascination with Robert Heinlein. After my father came home, I would go out and play for an hour or so. After supper we all listened to the radio until my parents went to bed. After that, I would read until one or two o'clock in the morning. Next day, sleep late, get up, and repeat the previous day. It was becoming more obvious that Mom's condition was worsening. The pain was increasing, in spite of medication. She even began to complain, which she had never done before. After my 15th birthday, near mid-August, she took an overdose of pain pills. There was no surprise, and little time remained. She was institutionalized because she was deemed suicidal. I did not see her. I think it was decided that I should not, but, for whatever reasons, I did not. We two, who had virtually never been apart, would never speak again. In October she died and the separation was made permanent. There was no farewell. I was bereft.

My father, who liked nothing better than being the cynosure of attention, attended to the funeral arrangements. I was particularly unhappy that he decided that we would have two wakes, one in Buffalo and another in

New York City, where she was to be buried with my sister in the Kane family plot in St. Raymond's Cemetery in the Bronx. I thought it cruel that I had to endure two separate wakes, two days of sitting and listening to other people talk about her. Retrospectively, he was correct because the wake in New York City was both convenient and appropriate for her sisters, whereas Buffalo, followed by a funeral mass and interment in the Bronx, would have imposed a needless burden on them. All of them resided either in the Bronx or in northern New Jersey. As we all do in cases of necessity, I coped. I even took some pride that, in the approved stoic male model of the era, I only cried once, as we followed the coffin down the aisle after the funeral mass. Privately I was less philosophic.

After the funeral we returned to Buffalo, my father to work and me to school. Shortly after our return my father auctioned off virtually all of our household goods and possessions. I was present at the auction and on several occasions asked that individual items I particularly associated with my mother be withdrawn as keepsakes for purely sentimental reasons. My father was, at least on that day, a stern man of business. Not one item was reserved. Sentiment was not negotiable.

We settled in to an awkward, quasi-distant relationship. I kept house – or, at least I cooked and did some cleaning. We ate a lot of veal after I discovered veal chops broiled quite nicely and that the broiling pan cleaned up relatively easily. We saw relatively little of each other, between work and school. Then, in the evening, pretty much as had always been the norm, he was prone to step out for a beer or three. I think he was trying, but unsure as to what he needed to do. On one interesting occasion, he happily gave me two handsomely bound books which he had acquired from a drinking companion. I am sure he thought *The Arabian Nights* a wonderful choice for a fifteen-year-old boy. When I discovered that it was an unexpurgated edition, so did I. The other volume, of which he knew nothing, was even more exciting. It was *The Decameron* by Boccaccio. Few teenage boys of that period (or any other) ever received books that were that bawdy in nature from their fathers. Until the day he died, I don't think he ever knew.

After my mother's death, changes took place in the way in which I lived my life. I now had more time to linger after school, to associate with or to make friends. I began to regularly attend the games played by the school teams (the Timon Tigers). As we entered 1951, I was at most basketball games, at home or away, then at baseball games in the spring. I started to hang out and help out at the athletic department and, as a senior, I would become the student manager of the football team. It was a happy association in which I was fully involved, even though in a peripheral role. In addition to the formal activities, practices and games, there were also social activities and one-on-one or small group gatherings over cokes or sodas. It also brought me into further contact with adults: coaches, trainers and others. My favorite history teacher, Father Arnold Brown, was the moderator of the football team and I valued the additional opportunity to "hang out" with him. Each week, we shared a particular task. On Monday, after school, we would collect the team's game uniforms (soiled over the weekend) and take them to Shanley's dry cleaners. They were transported in one or two large canvas laundry carts mounted on casters. We loaded the carts into the back of a pickup truck and drove to the cleaners. One Monday, for no particular reason, I decided to ride over in one of the carts. Father Arnold, who was at that time himself quite a young man, began to accelerate and decelerate in such a manner that the cart would roll and bang into the back of the cab. We were both enjoying the game when he began to turn the corner for Shanley's. Had he been a physicist rather than an historian, he might have allowed more for inertia than he did. Or at least that the wheels on the cart were swivels. The laundry cart obeyed the laws of physics and it, and I and a cart full of uniforms followed an eccentric path which took us to, and over the side, of the truck just ahead of the right rear wheel.

I have heard it said that, when faced with deadly peril, one sees one's life flash before his eyes. I am not sure how deadly the peril was, though it surely felt terrifying – but all that flashed before my eyes was the sight of a very large, black, tire moving inexorably toward me as I moved toward it. Once again, the laws of physics and/or the luck of the Irish were at work, and I hit the pavement somewhere between a few inches and a foot beyond the wheel. Father Arnold made a panic stop and was at my side almost before I had gotten off the ground. The adrenalin was flowing and I was, on the one hand, busy pretending that I had not been frightened, and on the other actually exultant that I seemed to be "sound in wind and limb." Father Arnold was concerned about me, but I assured him that apart from badly scraped palms from breaking my fall, I was OK. He kept seeking reassurance as we retrieved and delivered the uniforms and returned to school. (I did not ride back in the laundry cart.) He even suggested that I might want to take the next one or two days off. I made light of the experience and it was, after all, in the end, trivial. So, I just went back to school. I think I was several years older before I realized that in addition to his real concern for me he also had his own, adult concerns. He had been playing a childish and dangerous game with me and the truck. He was responsible, morally and legally, for me. His immediate superiors would certainly have been irate had the outcome of our adventure been less fortunate. Knowing what I have come to know, I might just have taken that day or two off – though I really had no use for a day or two at home, alone.

I also took up smoking in this period. The first day I smoked, I smoked an entire package of cigarettes. Naturally, I was terribly light-headed and nauseous. Still, I discovered that I liked to smoke. Perhaps it had something to do with the fact that my mother and father were both heavy smokers. It has also been suggested that somehow, psychologically, it had something to do with my mother's death. I have no idea about any of that. I do know that I began a twenty-year smoking habit which would see me work my way through three packages of cigarettes or more each day for two decades. I thought little about it, perhaps because my parents had accustomed me to it. As "modern" parents, they had always said, "If you want to smoke, just let us know. You don't need to sneak around." That attitude was, I am sure, what they believed to be enlightened and sophisticated. Anyway, for whatever reasons and/or contributing factors, I was now a smoker.

I was a high school junior when my mother died. The Korean War had begun a few months before her death. As my passage through high school went on, from Biology to Chemistry to Physics, so too the war. I was aware of the cost of war; my 1951-52 yearbook (my senior year), memorialized John Sanger, USMC, Timon 1950, KIA Korea, Nov. 1951, less than a year-and-a-half after his graduation. Nevertheless, sometime between the autumn of 1950 and the spring of 1952, I determined that if the war was still being fought when I graduated, I would enlist. That determination became a keystone in the arch of my adolescent thinking. Equally important was the decision that, after I left the Army, I would go to college and prepare myself to become a professor of history. In fact, I think that decision had been made much earlier – perhaps when Sister Anne Marie first introduced me to the American Revolution. Oddly enough for adolescent decision-making, that was precisely the path that I did, in fact, pursue.

The transfer from Syracuse to Buffalo had not proven to be as productive or lucrative as my father had hoped. While Buffalo was then a thriving industrial city, with steel mills and grain mills and chemical and other industrial activities, the grass seemed to be no greener for my father than it had been in Syracuse. If our economic status improved, it was only marginally – though I suppose that after my mother's death there were somewhat larger amounts of disposable income. The monies from the sale of the Bronx property were long gone and my father's dreams of greener pastures and greater prosperity now became focused on New York City. As we moved into 1951 he began, at first subtly, then more overtly to hint at, and then to discuss, plans for a move to "the City." I had adapted to our changed situation and family structure, but I was happy at Timon and with my own circle of friends and acquaintances. I am sure that a psychologist could expound learnedly about the impact of my mother's death, the near constant upheavals since 1947, a need for stability, and so on. I only knew that I did not want to move again. Another new school, in the fall of 1951, would be my sixth or seventh in five years. Two in the last year in Syracuse, Our Lady of Victory in Lackawanna, Saranac Lake High, back to OLVA, Timon and now??? I vigorously objected. My father suggested a compromise. We would effect an amicable separation. My father would move to New York City, or environs, and I would stay in Buffalo. We located an elderly widow, called Mrs. Byington, who had an attic room to rent. She and my father reached an agreement on a monthly payment for room and board and, when school started, he left for New York City (or at least the metropolitan area). I, meanwhile, moved into a large and comfortable attic room (though as with all attic rooms overly warm in late summer) for my senior year. Physically and psychologically, if not economically, I was on my own. I do not believe that I missed my father; nor do I have any reason to believe that he missed me. So, mentally I began my independent existence.

In the academic year 1951-52, I was sixteen years old and probably one of the least supervised adolescents in New York State. Mrs. Byington was a warm and friendly woman who seemed to enjoy my company, was happy to have me join her watching television, and she even shared her cigarettes with me if I ran short. Today, I suspect, she might have had to fear mob action if such a horror came to light. I think the only cross words we ever had related to the then ubiquitous professional wrestling shows, which she loved. I ventured, with the pure arrogance of youth, to inform her that the bouts were clearly rigged and not worthy of watching. (Though I must confess that I did have a sneaking affection for a character known as "Yukon Erik.") It took her several days to forgive me, and I think I learned a useful lesson about respecting other people's affection for things trivial and "letting sleeping dogs lie." In any event, in the aftermath, "Gorgeous George" and "Yukon Erik" and all the rest went forward to fame and fortune and I, I hope, became more tactful – or at least learned when to shut up. The old Latin adage *De gustibus non est disputandum* (In matters of taste, there ought to be no dispute), became a part of my vocabulary from that time on.

The school year was great fun. I had more free time than I had ever had and I spent most of it at school. The atmosphere was, I think, particular to that time. I had earlier mentioned what I referred to as "Catholic triumphalism" in this historical period. American Catholicism had arrived. While there were still those who feared and hated Catholicism (Protestants and Others United for the Separation of Church and State comes to mind), Catholic themes and figures were prominent in popular culture. Films such as *The Fighting 69th* and *Going My Way* celebrated Catholic sensibility and spirituality but also more individualistic virtues such as compassion and courage. Stars, such as Jimmy Cagney, Pat O'Brien and Bing Crosby were guaranteed to fill the seats of theatres. Notre Dame's football teams dominated sports reporting in an era when most collegiate teams were perceived as local or regional, and only Notre Dame and Army and Navy fielded teams which automatically commanded national interest. Catholic churches were packed at three or four masses every Sunday, and young men and women flocked to study for the priesthood or as brothers or nuns. At Timon, in my senior year, twenty-five of thirty members of the faculty were priests. I have discussed them as teachers, but they were also fully functioning as priests, a role which we understood. For example, on Friday afternoon, after the last class many of us did not simply rush out of the building. Rather, after dismissal, many of the friars returned to their homerooms and many of the boys would seek out one or another to go to confession. Catholics were urged to receive Holy Communion, the central act of the Catholic faith, frequently, and for many the confession of sin and its absolution, with an appropriate penance was a necessary first step. If you went to confession at school, there was no need to go Saturday afternoon at church when the lines might be long. The notion that your confessor might also teach you algebra was of no consequence, on either side. No one ever was concerned that the seal of the confessional might be violated just because the confessional was your homeroom.

In extracurricular activities the friars were virtually omnipresent. Whether it was the school paper, the yearbook, debate, radio or theatre, a friar served as moderator, coach, tutor or advisor. In addition to supervising and/or advising, they were not infrequently involved in painting a stage flat or teaching or researching a necessary skill or technique. In each case, the activity brought them closer to their students. I suspect it would be useful here, in the light of the scandals of the latter 1960s and 1970s, which have recently marred the reputation of the priesthood, to note that in all my associations with priests throughout my youth, I was not only never exposed to a scintilla of illicit intrigue; I never even heard of such a thing. We were often close to our faculty and not infrequently confided in them (as opposed to confession), and we never, in any way, found them threatening. Well, maybe in one way; it was not unknown for a friar to quickly cuff a young man he thought stood in need of correction.

I have spoken little here about girls. Not because they did not interest me. Primarily, the reason is that I had very little contact with girls in my age group during this period. I had my first "date" in Syracuse, when I was ten or eleven. It seems ungallant, but I no longer remember her name. We went to a YMCA dance where we both proved to be somewhat less than adept at learning the Virginia Reel. After what seemed to me to be a very pleasant evening, we took the bus back home and went to her house, where her mother served apple cider and cookies. After that I thanked her and her mother, left and walked home. It was not long after this that the game of musical towns and musical schools, which occupied so much of my life between 1946 and 1949, began. In that time, I was rarely in one place long enough to know a girl well enough to ask her out. I had a great crush in my last few months in Syracuse, on a girl I'll call Kate Mahoney. She had wonderful red hair, lots of freckles, and she smiled and laughed a lot, and I thought the sun rose and set on her. The result was a great deal of chatting – I remained confident as long as the topics were impersonal. Anything other than that reduced me to the stereotypical teenaged stumbling idiot. When we got to Lackawanna, I encountered another red-headed girl – with a similar result. (My wife, by the way, would prove to be a strawberry blonde.) Then, we were off to Saranac Lake, then back to Lackawanna and then to Timon. Some of my social awkwardness certainly had to do with the fact that I was a full year younger than my classmates and was among the smaller boys; some of my difficulties had to do with the fact that I didn't stay still long enough to develop female friends and contacts, but most were due to my personal shyness and feelings of inadequacy. I think I felt myself not particularly attractive or estimable and assumed that girls were likely to see through me as clearly as I did. Certainly the Timon years provided few opportunities to expand my dating circle and, even if they had, I doubt I would have shown greater aplomb or sophistication. My greatest social interactions of those years tended to be a brief encounter over a "coke" or a milkshake. Guys I knew often boasted that they could get girls to go with them for a "timber float" (a glass of water with a toothpick floating in it). I never developed that level of self-confidence.

In any event, there is little to recount of interest in my "social life" in those years. This is not to suggest that I was unaware of girls. Little could be farther from the fact. The female of the species fascinated me to an astonishing degree. I even noted that, in those pre-backpack days, boys and girls carried their schoolbooks differently. Boys usually carried their books, balanced on a three ring binder, on their hips. Girls also balanced their books on a binder, but carried them in both arms, under their breasts. However, like an anthropologist with a strange and puzzling tribe, that merely left me with facts I had noted, but with no hypothesis upon which to act.

In any event, between class work and assisting with sports teams and talking and laughing with friends, as well as an hour or so a day with Mrs. Byington, my senior year passed happily and quickly and suddenly graduation was upon us. My graduation day was somewhat unusual. My father had come up from New Rochelle, in Westchester County, where he was living, for the ceremony. As was then the custom, the graduation was held in the school's auditorium. We processed in (though caps and gowns were not then *de rigueur* for high school graduations but were reserved for baccalaureate ceremonies) and sat down. The usual ceremonies, rituals and awards were celebrated and diplomas were presented. My father had carefully prepared. We walked out of the hall, picked up my suitcase, which had been stored in some office and walked out of the building for the last time. We went to the railroad depot, boarded a train and left for metropolitan New York. I don't think I missed the graduation parties so much, but I would have preferred to linger, saying goodbyes. I would see none of my classmates again until our 50th Class Reunion. That evening, I entered New Rochelle for the first time. It would be my legal residence for the next eleven years. For the first time in my life I had at least a limited claim on being a "New Yorker" in the imperial sense.

Having started school just after my fourth birthday, I was still only sixteen when I graduated from high school, two months shy of my seventeenth birthday. My plan still called for me to enlist in the army as soon as possible. That required me to be seventeen and have my father's signed consent. Parental consent was a given. Effectively, however, my plans were on hold for two months, until mid-August. Because I was now in New Rochelle, I found myself in real proximity to both sides of the family. My father, who had been born in Braddock, Pennsylvania, in 1906, by this time had one surviving brother, his identical twin, Joe, and two sisters, Marjorie and Joan. Those three lived in Norwalk, Connecticut, a relatively short trip on the New York, New Haven and Hartford RR, which also served New Rochelle. As we have seen, his sister Lillian lived in Saranac Lake. His brother Art had died when I was about twelve. My mother had been born in "the City" in 1910 and was then survived by her sisters, Kitty, Anne, Margie and Monica. She had been predeceased by her brother Terrance and her sister Agnes. Two of my surviving aunts lived in Rutherford, New Jersey, Kitty and Margie: Anne and Monica lived close to one another in the Bronx. I had three cousins in Connecticut, all much younger than I, and also had three Kane cousins in New Jersey and four in the Bronx. (I omit here references to my Kelly side cousins in Saranac Lake and Port Henry, since they do not figure in the period under discussion. In all, they form another dozen.) In the next two months I was to see more of the Kanes than I ever had before and of the Kellys than I had since we were all in Syracuse. At sixteen, with two months to go before the army, I had few or no opportunities to work, and not a great deal of interest. I was living with my father in the usual second or third floor flat, and neither of us was enchanted with the other's company. The result was to be that I spent a great deal of time visiting my extended family.

The Kane girls, my mother's sisters, formed a tight, often stoical, but loving, group. They were so undemonstrative that my mother used to say that when you gave a Kane a gift, the only way to tell if they really liked it was to watch them. They would all express gratitude appropriately, but if they were really pleased they would, from time to time go back to the gift and touch or stroke it. Kitty was the oldest and was deferred to as a sort of matriarch. She formed half the Rutherford group with her husband, Charlie Murphy, and their children Jerry and Elna. Jerry was a navy veteran from World War II. My mother and I had traveled during the war to his "boot camp" (Sampson, near Geneva, New York) to visit him during his training. Elna, who was also older than I, I remember best from earlier visits, when she was a rather complete bobbysoxer, playing Sinatra records and brooding. She was a small girl, a Kane characteristic. Kitty and Charlie always provided a warm welcome, and I very much enjoyed visiting them. My Aunt Margie and her husband, Jack Bradley (who worked for RCA and was involved in the very early technical development of television) also lived in Rutherford, with their daughter Maureen, who was a delightful, laughing girl, a year or two younger than I. My mother and Margie were quite close in age and had apparently always been close, dating back to their days at Holy Angels. She was a wonderful repository of stories about my mother and exceptionally proud of all things Kane. A few years later, when I returned from Korea, I was having supper with Margie and Jack, and the meat course involved steak or chops – something that had a bone in it. As I worked with my knife and fork to separate the meat from the bone, Jack said, "don't worry Tom, just pick it up and eat it." I said thanks, but I was OK. Margie then said, *apropos* Kanes and manners, "He wouldn't do that, Jack; he's a Kane."

In the Bronx dwelt my Aunt Anne and Aunt Monica, each with two children. Anne, who was second in birth order, would succeed Kitty as matriarch. She and her husband, Vin Burns, had two children: young Vin, who was a few years older than I, and his sister Judith, who was born the same year I was, 1935. Probably because of the age factor, I was always closer to Judith than any of my other cousins, as we remain today. Monica and her husband, Bert Weaver, also had two children, Bobby and Kathy, who were ten or more years younger than I. Bobby was, for a few years, a child model, with at least one ad that ran nationally and was carried in most of the popular magazines of the day, to the substantial delight of his aunts. Monica was the last of the Kane girls and, as the baby at Holy Angels, had been much cosseted by the nuns. As an adult, she possessed a gift for *repartee* which extended up to (or down to) a real New York wisecrack. Unlike her sisters, she continued to work after her children were born, and Bobby and Kathy had a live-in nanny who stayed with the family after the children were grown; indeed, until her death.

In those two months, I visited all my mother's sisters, always staying either at Kitty's or Anne's home. However, it was primarily with the Norwalk Kellys that I spent my time, particularly with my father's twin, Joe. Joe had married after World War II. His wife was a wonderful woman named Elva and they had a very young son named Michael. Marjorie was also married, to a truck driver named Bill Surrette, and they had two daughters named Mary Marjorie and Kathleen. All three cousins were much younger than I. Bill was a World War II veteran, a combat engineer, who had seen a lot of combat and, who, unlike most of the veterans I have known in the ensuing sixty or so years, had actually liked combat and rather relished the killing of the enemy. I assume he had met Marjorie through Joe, whose career involved the management of trucking companies. It was an odd pairing, the petite, classical music-oriented soprano and the very large, hard-drinking, totally blue collar truck driver. It almost seemed like a pilot for a situation comedy. For a sixteen-year-old, Norwalk sometimes seemed like another world. Joe too was a World War II veteran, though he had not seen combat. Both were pillars of their local *American Legion* post and were, if not happy, at least willing, to have me follow them around. I did so with pleasure, regarding it as a sort of rite of passage into both the military and manhood.

Norwalk also (more properly Joe's house) was the first place I had ever sort of regularly semi-inhabited that had television. (Mrs. Byington had television but I went there only by invitation.) In Norwalk, I had access to a TV set, afternoons free and a virtually unlimited number of *Brooklyn Dodgers* baseball games to watch. As was true for most of my generation, my affection for baseball began on vacant lots. We all played, no matter how poorly. I was, perhaps particularly inept, at least until we discovered, in sixth grade, that I was quite spectacularly nearsighted. I had always sat in the front seats but Sister Blanche believed in alphabetical seating and we quickly discovered that from the seats toward the back of the room, I saw little except vague motion. Glasses not only improved my game, they enabled me to view the field as it should be seen. The *Syracuse Chiefs* of the old, Triple A, International League, known as the "high minors," was my first love and, just after the war they had excellent teams and some players, such as pitcher Herm Wehmeier and outfielder Hank Sauer who would perform at a high level in the major leagues. Indeed, Sauer in 1952, as a *Chicago Cub*, would be chosen MVP with 37 home runs and 121 RBIs. When we moved to Buffalo, the *Buffalo Bisons* replaced the *Chiefs* in my baseball pantheon.

These were the glory days of New York baseball, when the *Yankees,* the *Dodgers* and the *Giants* dominated the sport. I was enamored of the *Dodgers*, later immortalized by Roger Kahn as *The Boys of Summer.* What a team they were: Gil Hodges, Jackie Robinson, Pee Wee Reese, Billy Cox, Roy Campanella, Duke Snider, Carl Furillo. Preacher Roe, Don Newcomb and all the others. It was an affection I would never lose.

Between Rutherford and the Bronx and Norwalk and baseball and the *American Legion* bar, the two months passed quickly. Suddenly, on Wednesday, August 13th 1952, I was seventeen, though there was no fanfare. New Rochelle had one recruiting office for all the armed forces, staffed, as it happened, by an Air Force non-commissioned officer. I presented myself there on either the thirteenth or fourteenth of August. The airman and I filled out the preliminary paperwork for a three-year enlistment in the United States

Army. I was given the necessary papers for my father to sign, giving consent for me to serve in the armed forces of the United States, and I agreed to return the next day to complete the enlistment. I did so. The Air Force NCO added my father's consent to the stack of forms, stapled them together and showed me where to sign. For some reason, I hesitated. I was certainly not suspicious of anything; why should I be? While I hesitated, my eyes were skimming the papers presented to me. That was sufficient to alert me to the fact that I was about to agree to serve *four years in the United States Air Force*. Had it gone unchanged, that bit of chicanery would have altered my entire life. I would not have met and fallen in love with the woman I was to marry, my children would not exist and, who knows what else would have happened? I quite angrily insisted that proper papers be drawn up for a three-year, *Army* enlistment, left, and returned later and enlisted. I was then told, somewhat curtly as I recall, to present myself at the induction center, on Whitehall St. in NYC on the following Tuesday. So I began the next phase of my life.

CHAPTER 5
Me and the Last Days of the Brown Shoe Army

Whitehall Street in Manhattan was the induction center for the metropolitan area. In addition to people like me who had enlisted, it was also the place where young men whose local draft boards had selected them for two years compulsory service reported for their physical examinations and initial processing. Those physical and psychological and intellectual examinations determined whether or not they would be rejected or would report for active duty. As such, it was a very busy place. In those days, active duty soldiers were divided into two classes. You were either US or RA. The reference was to the prefix to your military serial number. If you were drafted, you had an obligation to serve for two years on active duty with a two-year commitment to an active reserve unit and two years in the inactive reserve, and your serial number began with the prefix US. If you were a volunteer, you served three years on active duty, with a three-year reserve commitment (though none in the active reserves), and your serial number began with RA (RA 12345678). The RA stood for "Regular Army."

In addition to the physicals, prospective soldiers were also subjected to a series of psychological tests and questions, the most famous (or notorious) of which, designed to deny entry to homosexuals, was the penetrating question, "do you like girls?" There was also an intelligence test, the AGCT test, which altered my path in the army and, possibly, in life. I had enlisted with "no specification," which at that time usually meant assignment to a combat arm: infantry, artillery or armor. After the AGCT test, I was interviewed or counseled, or some such, but in any event I left Whitehall Street destined for service in the Army Security Agency which was, and I assume still is, the Army's equivalent of the National Security Agency. Whatever else that may have done, the extensive schooling required after basic training insured that I would not arrive in Korea until just after the July 1953 armistice brought an end to the Korean War.

At the end of that quite long day, I was sworn into service and sent home. I think we reported a day or two later and were shipped to Camp Kilmer, New Jersey. I might note here that I will be mentioning a number of military posts: some "Camps" and some "Forts." In 1952, "Forts" were considered *permanent* installations and "Camps" were *temporary.* Located in New Jersey, Kilmer had been named for the World War I era poet who had been killed fighting in France with the old 69th New York Infantry Regiment (165th Infantry, 42nd Division) in World War I. A convert to Catholicism, Joyce Kilmer was a name well-known in all Catholic educational and literary circles at that time.

Here we underwent initial processing, drawing uniforms, boots, a duffle bag and the other necessary *impedimenta,* designed to at least outwardly convert us from civilians to soldiers. Here was administered the brutally short haircut that had been a target for humorists since the draft was started in 1940. Since I already was sporting a crew cut I did not fall under the scissors of the Kilmer barbers. The haircut, like the uniforms and equipment was, in essence, identical to that issued to our older brothers and cousins in the later stages of World War II. There was one exception. Even their underwear was OD; our t-shirts and boxer shorts were white. We were issued a heavy brown woolen Eisenhower or "Ike" jacket, which was cut off and cinched at the waist, with brown woolen trousers to match. The color was, officially, OD (olive drab). Unofficially, it was called "s—t brindle brown." This together with a khaki shirt and a dark tie and khaki socks and brown "low quarter" shoes—an actual shoe, rather than a boot—was the prescribed winter uniform. It also included an "overseas cap" of the same material. At rest, this formed a nearly rectangular object about 11 inches in length by 5½ in height. It opened for wear and could be cocked at a very rakish angle, though regulations required that it be worn straight upon the head.

For summer wear, we wore the same light tan khaki shirts as in winter (there were then no short sleeve shirts for summer wear), matching khaki trousers, khaki ties and service caps. The khaki shirts and trousers, after cleaning and pressing, would be returned so heavily starched that, if the trouser legs were spread apart, they could be made to stand up in a triangle. Winter and summer, the uniform required a web belt, in khaki, with a large brass buckle, which required frequent polishing with a brass cleaning agent. For training and details, we were issued fatigue uniforms and two pair of boots. The fatigues were green and loose fitting and the boots were brown. The boots, taken together with the low quarter shoes were, of course, the origin of the use of the term *Brown Shoe Army rmy* as a faint pejorative, by the 1960s Army (whose shoes and boots were black), to describe the Army of the '50s. When processing and the issuing of uniforms were completed, we were sent through a line which led to a photographer. There, dressed in our summer khaki (it was after all August) and posed with an American flag, we were photographed. Copies were available for purchase.

Then came additional processing and sorting. For example, those who were assigned to the infantry were assigned to sixteen-week basic training courses. Those of us designated for specialized training, whether the ASA, or pole lineman school or cooks and bakers school, were slotted for eight weeks of basic training. Depending on the result of the sorting, we were then assigned to so-called transient barracks, that is, temporary quarters. Thus began a long exposure to squad bays and barracks life.

The next morning brought my real introduction to army life. I don't remember the hour at which I heard my first reveille, but I do remember the scene which ensued. I found myself in the midst of sixty or so young men, none of whom I had ever seen prior to the previous day. All were clad, as they had slept, in boxer shorts and t-shirts. The squad bay was engulfed in a verbal storm of vulgarity and obscenity (see below), a fusillade of farting, more scratching than seemed reasonable or necessary and a cumulative drift toward the latrine (Army for bathroom). That consisted of eight or ten commodes, all in a row, with not even a vague effort at separation or privacy. In some barracks which I would inhabit in years to come, there would be individual urinals, in others merely a communal trough at which one staked out his place. We would come to realize that individual privacy was not regarded as standard issue in the United States Army. Indeed, it was nonexistent. The showers were equally communal: one large room with a number of individually controlled shower heads. There were individual sinks for washing, shaving, brushing teeth and so forth, located down one wall of the same room which housed the commodes and urinals. We would also quickly learn that, at least for the immediate future, whether in regard to bodily functions or ablutions, **rapidity** was not only recommended, it was requisite.

This is probably as good a place as any to deal with the casual, if nearly obsessive, use of vulgarity by soldiers of that time. Blasphemy, in a literal if unthinking manner, was as common as asking for a drink of water. Vulgarity, particularly the use of common Anglo-Saxon forms of sexual organs, both male and female was rife, along with other traditional forms of humor and abuse. The more scatological the term or phrase, the greater the use. What is now called, "the F word" was the King-Emperor of the soldier's lexicon. Sometimes, obscenity and or misogyny was simply a portion of our training. The rhyming form of cadence counting while being taught to march was such an instance. One, fairly printable example of such a rhyme, was "I know a girl, All dressed in black, She makes her living, On her back. Sound off, One two, Sound off, Three four ...." On one occasion, while I was in Korea, I made a whimsical bet that I could get through an entire day, unless speaking to officers, without using any word, other than the "F word, though with variations in tone and emphasis. I used and abused the word in its adjectival and adverbial forms, as noun and verb and in all possible variations from the dawn of the day through the afternoon. My experiment ultimately failed when I was suddenly accosted and responded without thinking. Still. I rested content, and amused, with the knowledge that the concept was credible even though its implementation was flawed. I cannot speak to current usage though I suspect that the addition of huge numbers of women to the Army has done less to alter the Army's use of language than to corrupt the usage of female soldiers, if indeed that was necessary in the 21st Century.

Normally, soldiers passing through Camp Kilmer for initial assignment were there only two or three days. In my case something apparently went wrong and I was there significantly longer, perhaps a week or ten days. That additional time would expose me to two experiences, one negative and one positive, which had some influence on my life in the Army and on my life written larger. The first lesson I learned was that for a low ranking enlisted man (and at that time, as a private, E-1, I was the lowest of the low) being unassigned but physically available, in transient status, was a thoroughly abysmal situation. You were not assigned to any organization on the post, but you were physically available for duties, such as KP (kitchen police – everything from cleaning out garbage cans with a steam hose, to washing huge pots and pans, to dishing out food, mopping floors, etc.). So, on my first Sunday in the Army, I drew K.P.

We (the KPs) all reported to the mess hall at about 0500 hours (the Army uses a 24 hour clock, so there is no 5 a.m. and 5 p.m. but 0500 and 1700 hours) and began our assigned duties. About 0800, I approached the Mess Sergeant and asked when I might be relieved so that I could attend Mass. He told me to forget it, that I was on KP all day. I reminded him that under regulations, I had the right to attend church (which was true). He told me, in somewhat less delicate language, that I could go whistle up a rope. If I had been stationed at Kilmer, I could have pursued the issue. As a transient, as he well knew, there really was no recourse. He thereupon assigned what I am sure he regarded as "the smart mouth kid" to several hours of cleaning garbage cans with a steam hose. While certainly negative, the experience was not entirely without value. It was an early lesson in learning to pick my battles. In future, when I was in transient status, I would carefully guard my position, often quite successfully. (See below.)

The positive experience came from the men with whom I shared a barracks in those few days. They were, in a classic sense, a motley crew. Here I was, seventeen, an upstate New Yorker, a Catholic and an RA. Among them, all draftees, there was a college graduate from a distinguished mid-Western university. He had been the president of the local chapter of The Young Progressives League in college. He had instituted civil suit against the commandant of Camp Kilmer claiming he was being held against his will, in violation of the U.S. Constitution. There were also two or three other young men, vaguely of the "left," who were engaged in various ploys designed to find a loophole which would get them out of the Army.

There was also a young man who was suffering badly from some form of arthritis who should never have been inducted into service. We all knew he would get out, but while with us, he actually was physically suffering. He was put on KP (he was a transient) and spent half a day in a steam-filled room, cleaning pots and pans. It was painful over the next two days to watch him recover. There were others, to a total of perhaps eight or ten. As transients, if we were not detailed for specific duties, we had no place to be and no duties to fulfill.

There were no radios or television sets in barracks in those days, so, we talked – and talked, and talked. We debated the existence of God, the legitimacy of the draft, the Constitution of the United States and the wisdom of the Cold War in general and the Korean War in particular. In most of the discussions, I was in the minority, if not standing alone. Most of the others had college degrees, or at least some time in college. At least in rhetorical skills, that fact meant much more two generations ago than it does today. My primary recollection of those few days of argument is how generous they were. They did not yield an iota of their positions but would often offer me suggestions and tactical or mechanical pointers that might strengthen my ability if not my case. I have, of course, long since realized that I became something of a mascot for them but they were always civil, always courteous and always generous. I like to think that I learned from them.

Finally, whatever had held me at Kilmer was overcome and I received orders to report to Fort Dix (also in New Jersey) for eight weeks of basic training. I was assigned to B Battery, 34th Field Artillery Battalion, 60th Infantry Regiment, 9th Infantry Division. I should note here that all training was as infantry. We were denominated a field artillery battery, but other than the title the battery trained as did the infantry companies that formed the regiment. We were bussed from Camp Kilmer to Fort Dix and training began. By now it was late summer, 1952.

President Truman had ordered the military services to desegregate in 1948, but it was not until the exigencies of the Korean War pressed that that process was accelerated. By this time, it was largely complete. Our basic training instructors (the cadre) illustrated that well. While very few of the recruits in my platoon were men of color, certainly not more than 3-5%, **all** of our senior non-commissioned officers were African-American – then still called Negroes. On the other hand, **none** of our commissioned officers were. Both the proximity of Negro recruits and the authority of Negro instructors were new and strange to virtually all of us. On the other hand, I don't ever remember it being remarked upon, even by the more overtly racist among us.

My platoon sergeant, whom we will call Sgt. Badger, was from the Deep South. Physically, he was about average height and build and was usually soft spoken. My first memory of him was of all of us gathered around as he demonstrated how to make a bunk to military specifica-tions. (In theory the blanket on a properly made bunk is sufficiently taut that a coin dropped onto it will bounce up from the surface.) One of our recruits would have so much trouble in achieving this that, once he had achieved the requisite result, he refused to sleep in the bunk for a no-ticeable period of time. If one awoke in the middle of the night, he could be seen crouched on the footlocker at the foot of his bunk. It was as pitiable as it was amusing.

As the sergeant demonstrated, he sought to make some sort of contact with his trainees, asking "Who's the oldest man in this platoon?"

A Maine man answered: "I probably am, I'm twenty-six." Badger then asked who was the youngest man.

I responded, "I'm seventeen, sergeant."

He looked at me and said, "Boy, how'd you get so hard lookin' [*sic*] in seventeen years?" The platoon laughed, but my baby-faced self, not grasping his irony (probably because I *was* seventeen) accepted it at face value and was foolishly pleased. That same night, we were offered a novel spectacle, indeed a unique one in my three years on active duty. As we prepared for lights out, and washed and brushed our teeth in the latrine, one of the recruits emerged, ready for bed, clothed in red silk pajamas. The shouts of laughter and glee still ring in my ears. Suffice it to say that the sartorial display was never repeated.

We began with the school of the soldier. We learned how to salute properly, how to wear our uniforms, how to stand at attention and at parade rest. We learned facing movements: right face, left face, about face, etc. The Army, it seemed, had a way to perform every action and the Army way was the only acceptable way. We began to learn close order drill: marching up and down on one drill field or another and responding to commands ranging from "forward march," "to the left oblique, march," and culminating in something like "double to the rear by the left flank march." As we marched, we learned to respond as a unit, whether a squad, a platoon or a company. We were, though not consciously, learning the obedience of the soldier.

On one such day, my squad, with that Maine man as acting squad leader got separated as the other three squads of the platoon marched off. It was an honest error; we were confused as to whether or not we had been given orders and as we dithered, the opportunity to respond passed us by. After five or ten minutes Sgt. Badger returned in search of us and in a highly annoyed state. After berating us at some length, he announced that we would, forthwith, join the other squads but when the day's exercises were over, we would be required to double time (run) around the Company area until he got tired (all delivered in a rich regional and/or ethnic dialect I shall not attempt) and, he concluded, "and, Gentlemen, I ain't gonna be runnin'" [*sic*].

At that, Badger was unusually kind. It was not unknown for NCOs to force troops to run, wearing helmets without helmet liners. A helmet liner, fitted inside the steel helmet and contained webbing so that the liner, and hence the helmet, was "fitted" to the individual head. If required to wear the helmet without the liner and run, the trooper had to hold on to the helmet with one hand while running. The motion caused the "steel pot" to bounce up and down on his head while he ran which could really could hurt. Badger spared us that.

From individual skills, the school of the soldier, we moved to training in squads. At that time, an infantry squad in training was normally composed of a dozen men. There was a cumulative effect because as we moved along, we continued to be required to master new skills individually as well as to exercise them collectively. After squad training, we trained as a platoon, perhaps 60 to 75 men, and finally, as a company, around 250 men. We were housed in so-called temporary barracks, which had been built for the exigencies of World War II. Some, the story went, when reopened for Korean War usage (fighting Communism) still had posters on bulletin boards from c. 1945 extolling the virtues of the Soviet Army in that earlier war. Each consisted of two stories with a platoon on each floor. Picture a large rectangular space with 12 to 15 bunks on each side of a central aisle, and then, each bunk space doubled, by placing an upper bunk over the lower. Each trooper had a footlocker at the head of the bunks and limited space for hangers along the exterior wall, to hang his uniforms. Closed footlockers contained most uniforms, underwear, and provided seating space in off-duty hours, of which there were few.

A normal duty day was quite likely to extend from perhaps 0500 until 2100 or 2200 at night. Bodily functions, washing, shaving and showering for both platoons, were dealt with in the latrine, as previously described. There were private or semi-private rooms for the platoon sergeant and other non-coms assigned to the platoon. The upper story was partially supported by six or so vertical beams or posts, on each side of the central aisle, which ran from the foundation of the building to the roof. Each beam, on each floor, had a "butt can" nailed to it. Usually painted red and filled with sand, the butt cans were the safe repositories for cigarette butts as they were discarded. Since we were required to scrub the barracks floors at the conclusion of each week as a preliminary to Saturday morning's inspection, it would have required an exceptionally stupid or thoughtless man to stamp out a discarded cigarette on the barracks floor. A rotating barracks orderly saw to the disposal of the butts, replenishment of the sand, etc.

The Army was equally fastidious about disposing of cigarettes outdoors. Outside, if you wished to dispose of a cigarette butt, you were taught to "field strip" the butt. The cigarette paper was torn away from the tobacco, the tobacco dispersed on the ground and the paper, wadded into a tiny ball or wad, was either discarded or pocketed. This not only satisfied the Army's almost pathological quest for neatness and order, it also was good field craft because it left little or no evidence of troops passing by. In 1952, few smoked filtered cigarettes, though virtually everyone seemed to smoke. The Army field rations of the day, C rations, even provided each soldier with a mini package of four cigarettes per day.

Meals were provided and consumed at a Mess Hall, a large, utilitarian building designed to serve meals to hundreds of men in a minimum amount of time. As a general rule, wherever I served it would be fair to say that the food, while hardly inspired, was wholesome and prepared and served in reasonably sanitary conditions. Indeed, when assigned to KP, we provided the raw cleaning power of the culinary operation. Once again, as in World War II, we performed the same chores as had our older brothers, with one notable exception: by 1952, no one peeled potatoes anymore; machines had assumed that chore. It was not home cooking. Many young troopers were fascinated, many others revolted, when first confronted with SOS for breakfast. The dish consisted of ground beef, swimming in a gray, semi-liquid mass which was, I believe, intended to be either a white sauce or a white gravy. It was served on toast. The time-honored acronym stood for "S ..t on a Shingle." I personally had no aversion to it; indeed, I found it both tasty and nourishing. Since my mother had regularly served, not hamburger, but creamed chip beef on toast, the Army's coarser substitute did not seem strange to me. Whatever else may be said about it, it certainly did "stick to your ribs." The mess hall offered few culinary surprises. Most menu items were familiar and perfectly ordinary, and if the vegetables were boiled into mush, that was the way most of our mothers had served them anyway. (I am quite sure that at least another decade passed before I heard anyone say *al dente* out loud; in 1952, it was still primarily a crossword puzzle word.)

We were soon introduced to the basic infantry weapon of the old *Brown Shoe Army*, the M-1, Garand rifle. The M-1 was a gas operated, semi-automatic rifle. Contrary to much modern myth, a semi-automatic weapon does not continue to fire as long as a trigger is held down. It fires one shot at a time, one for each trigger pull. What makes it semi-automatic is that the gas generated by each shot drives the rod backwards, extracts the shell from the just fired round and inserts the next shell into the firing chamber. In short, having fired one shot, you could fire the next without having to work the bolt. It had been a significant development just prior to World War II, and it greatly increased the firepower of American infantry units during the war. Most infantry rifles of the World War II/Korean War era, like those of World War I, had rifle clips which held 3 to 5 rounds; the M -1 clip held eight.

We were instructed in the Manual of Arms: "Right shoulder arms," "Left shoulder arms," "Order arms," "Inspection arms," "Present arms" (a rifle salute). We learned to field strip the weapon – that is, to break it down into its component parts for cleaning and/or maintenance, to reassemble it and, in theory to know all its secrets. We did not, as some others did, learn to do that in the dark or blindfolded. We then went to a dry firing range (a place to exercise with the weapon but not to fire it).There we learned to aim, to control breathing while shooting, to squeeze, not pull, the trigger and various other techniques for effective use of the weapon. Since I had never fired a weapon prior to service, I found this instruction interesting.

Finally we were taken out to the post's rifle ranges to fire the weapons. By now we had been thoroughly indoctrinated with the proper nomenclature: it was a "rifle" not a "gun." For the army a "gun" is a crew served weapon. Thus a cannon or a machinegun, but not a shoulder arm or pistol. After limited practice, we began to fire for record. Firing for record involved shooting at large paper targets at various specified distances such as 100 yards or 300 yards. The latter was pretty much the effective killing range of the M-1 in the hands of an average soldier. The targets were raised and lowered from rifle pits (actually more like deep trenches). After you had fired on the target, the target was lowered and marked. That is, black adhesive patches were placed over the bullet holes in the target, which was then raised. The shooter was thus enabled to see where the shots he fired struck the target and adjust his shooting or the rifle's sights to compensate for any problem.

Firing was done from several positions, standing (offhand), kneeling, sitting and prone and at ranges from 100 to 300 yards. Ultimately, the shooter received a score; indeed, all troops engaged received a score. The most embarrassing moments of the day came from those men who missed the target completely. This was scored by the waving of a red flag or disc across the target, which was known as "Maggie's drawers." Those who qualified, were eligible for qualification badges: "Marksman", "Expert" and "Sharpshooter." Some guys had considerable difficulty and, since the troops did much of the scoring themselves, were rescued from their difficulty by the judicious use of what was known as the "M-1 pencil." That is, their scores were artificially adjusted upward.

The M-1 weighed about 9 pounds. When its bayonet was mounted, it weighed 10. A bayonet of that period was a long sword-like object ranging around 16-18 inches long, including both blade and hilt. Though seldom used (to the best of my knowledge, Americans made one bayonet charge during the Korean War, and that was the last to date), it remained a tactical possibility and so we were given training and practice, known as bayonet drill. American soldiers have never been fond of the bayonet; so a significant part of the exercise always seemed to me as much psychological as physical. We were taught to lunge and to parry and to use the butt of the rifle as a weapon, with a vertical or horizontal butt stroke and to remember not to thrust the blade too deeply into the enemy, lest it become stuck in his ribs. Throughout the drill, however, the instructor would shout, "What's a bayonet for?" and we would respond, lustily, "To kill!" He would then shout, "What are you?" and we would shout, "A killer!" This litany was frequently repeated during the drill. We were also required to shout when we thrust the bayonet, presumably into an enemy. I don't think it worked. Few of us took it seriously, other than the instructor. After all, we were off for cooks and bakers school or the ASA. Cold steel was much harder to envision than rifle fire. Personally, I found it faintly embarrassing.

Physical training—running, jumping, pushups, deep knee bends—was a part of every day. A formal PT session was held almost every morning, and the day was likely to see much double-timing, close order drill and other military exercises, up to and including twenty mile hikes with full packs. A few of the older draftees, from sedentary occupations, found some difficulty with the regimen. I was seventeen and though my leisurely summer until enlistment had been quite sedentary, youth carried the day. While sometimes tiring, the physical part of training represented no problem.

Some elements of training seemed more functional than others. After we had, at least in theory, attained weapons proficiency, we ran combat firing courses. Those featured pop-up targets at which we were to fire as rapidly as we could react to their appearance. I think most of us responded well to this element of our training. Somewhere, in a dresser drawer, I still have a metal ID bracelet, an item then popular, which has my name and serial number and an inscription "high squad combat firing … Battery B 34th F. A." which the Battery Commander and/or the battery's officers had paid for – 12 copies. It was certainly good for morale. I cherished it then and remember it fondly now.

We also understood, if we did not love, the utility of route marches, though I think no one has ever fondly reminisced about a twenty mile march with full packs. Our commanding officer, called Captain Gallagher, was a real foot soldier and wanted a better finishing time every time we did a long hike. It was not for nothing that we called him "Galloping" Gallagher. So, too, our bivouacs and field problems with pickets and patrols seemed clearly rational and brought little resentment. Some things seemed less probable and less functional, and when the Battery went to gas mask training (tear gas was used) some of us spent the afternoon playing cards in the barracks boiler room. We attended field lectures, seated in bleachers facing a field in which weapons or tactics could be demonstrated and explained. Some were informative and/or interesting; some soared beyond boring into the realm of insensibility.

A frequently overlooked part of military service in the latter half of the twentieth century was that, due to the draft, those of us who served had a virtually universal exposure to every type of male in the US: race, religion, ethnicity, political right or left, and all economic spheres. It made for an unusual and intensely broadening experience. Barracks bull sessions were often dull but sometimes enlightening. I remember one evening when the topic was sex. With an all-male and primarily single group of young men between 17 and 26, that was not unusual. As the chatting and inevitable boasting went on there was a sudden quiet comment from one of the few married men in the place. In a deep Southern drawl, he just calmly said, "sex ain't all it's cracked up to be." I'm still not sure exactly what his point was but he did succeed in totally altering the dynamic of the conversation. I learned a few things in barracks bull sessions. I learned a little about the life of an urban black male, and I discovered that I could befriend people from backgrounds about which I knew nothing, and gain knowledge as well as companionship. I also became aware of the multiplicity of experiences Americans enjoyed or endured.

In any event, in a sea of barracks BS and an ocean of drills and inspections, bivouacs and field problems, PT and marksmanship, eight weeks passed, and, in November, our training ended. (That November also saw the election of Dwight D. Eisenhower as president, for most of us, the first Republican president in our memory.) We had a "passing out" parade, a form of graduation, the only time in my years of service that the command "pass in review" was ever directed at me. It was our second parade – we had been detailed at one point to march in a sesquicentennial parade for some town in New Jersey. We were importuned by various Army groups (e.g., Airborne) to continue our career with them, and we received our orders for our next duty station. After a period of leave, I was to report to the Army Security Agency School in Fort Devens, Massachusetts, for a twenty-six week training period. I was to become a high speed Morse code radio intercept operator. We were no longer military preschoolers, we were now on our way to active duty, additional training or no.

I was to be at Fort Devens from December of 1952 to May of 1953. The "drill" on reporting was much the same as it had been at Fort Dix. We were assigned to school units, once again quartered in "temporary" barracks erected for World War II, and we were, once again, to be instructed and trained. Our training would include the usual pauses to swab down and scrub and clean the barracks for Saturday Inspection (the proverbial Friday night "GI Party") and we would pull details of various sorts, but primarily, we were students and, unlike basic training, at Devens we would, at least occasionally, get weekend passes. A weekend pass entitled the soldier who held it to leave the post after Saturday inspection (c. 1200) and remain at liberty until midnight on Sunday or until reveille on Monday morning. At the very least, one could go off-post for a drink or to try to meet a girl. We would do those things. In fact, as hard as it may be to believe in the 21st Century, with the near ubiquity of pizza parlors, I had my very first pizza on a Saturday night somewhere in the vicinity of Fort Devens. I don't think I had even heard of a pizza before.

Notable for its complete lack of weaponry, almost, except for our uniforms and barracks, a complete lack of any sense of the military, the ASA School was something less than inspiring. Dull as I found it, I had been brought up to understand that if you made your bed, you had to lie in it – and so I did.

The six months that I spent in Fort Devens in 1952-1953 was the least interesting period of my entire enlistment. Only my posting there after I returned from Korea even began to rival it. It is perhaps best described as boring to the *nth* degree. We began with a rather quickly taught introduction to Morse Code. Still in widespread use at this time, the Morse Code for wireless radio communications was derived from the code originated by Samuel F. B. Morse for use in telegraphic communications. It consisted of symbols (which represented sounds) used to signify the letters of the Latin alphabet and Arabic numbers. There were a few variants, but, since most military communications were sent in five member code groups, most often numbers, language variants were inconsequential. Morse symbols were written as a series of "dots" (-.. —- -) and "dashes" (-.. .- ... .). Thus, a transcribed "word" (code group) would appear on a typed page as 84914. Morse operators always spoke the symbols as "dits" and "dahs" because that was a fair approximation of the sound the operator heard. So, an operator who has spent too much time copying code, and is somewhat punchy as a result, may be said to be "dit" happy. (See Appendix A.)

During this era, sending messages in Morse was a much more reliable method of radio transmission than was voice communications. The reasons for that were primarily technical, but Morse communication was more reliable, less prone to produce garbled messages and capable of transmission and reception at significantly greater distances. In our own time, technological developments have essentially eliminated all of those impediments, and Morse has almost been eliminated, except among "ham" radio operators. Even the venerable ... —- ... (SOS) has been eliminated. In the 1950s, however, virtually all important military messages were encoded and then transmitted in Morse. The so-called People's Volunteer Army (PVA), the Red Chinese Army operating in Korea, transmitted all but the most mundane messages in five letter code groups, actually five number code groups. In transmission they used a standard Morse shortcut, using a shortened form of the Morse symbols for Arabic numbers, known as "cut numbers." (See Appendix A.) A quick example: a five-number group beginning with one and ending with five.

In full numbers one is .——— and five is …..: in cut numbers it becomes .- and then … thus saving a good deal of time, particularly in an extended message. In addition to the code itself, we were also required to memorize an extensive list of procedural signals. To mention a few by way of illustration: K indicated that the receiving station was prepared to receive your message; R, that the receiving station had received and acknowledged your message; AR, that the transmitting station had completed its traffic and CL, that the station was clear, that is was going off the air. There were, of course, scores and scores more, but these are, I think, adequate for illustration's sake.

We, the group to which I belonged, were to be trained as high speed Morse code radio intercept operators, (MOS), Military Occupational Specialty 1717. Other groups were to be trained for traffic analysis and cryptanalysis. Since we were to be intercept operators, that is, trained to listen to and copy enemy radio traffic, it was not necessary that we know how to transmit, and we received no such instruction. Nor were we taught or even told anything about traffic analysis and cryptanalysis. Traffic analysis is perhaps best illustrated with reference to the allied preparation for D-Day in 1944. To deceive the Germans, allied headquarters "created" a mythical First U. S. Army Group (FUSAG) ostensibly under the command of General George S. Patton. Through the use of a relatively few men, inflatable tanks and armored cars and aircraft and hours of radio traffic between "Armies" and "Corps" and "Divisions," as well as the normal "chatter" re Red Cross requests and USO shows for the troops, German traffic analysts were persuaded that a huge force existed in Northeastern England, prepared to invade the continent after the German Army rushed to repel the Normandy landings. Many lives were saved as German troop units remained in place waiting for the second landing.

Cryptanalysis is the actual "breaking" (decoding) of the enemy's radio traffic, so that you can actually "read" his traffic in real time. That is, to know what he is planning to do, even as he prepares to do it. That was the allied triumph of the codebreakers at Bletchley Park in England, which contributed so much to allied victory in World War II. The intercept operators were the underlying structure of all of this because it was they, copying enemy traffic, who provided access to the raw materials so brilliantly used by the analysts.

By the time of the Korean War, most military traffic was based on the use of "one time pads," which severely limited, if it did not completely frustrate, cryptanalysis. It is, in fact, unbreakable under almost all conditions. Since it is overly technical for this document, I refer the reader to the internet where many cogent explanations are available. There was no equivalent of Bletchley Park's triumph in the Korean War. The use of traffic analysis and radio direction finding, however, did perform militarily valuable tasks in Korea.

Once we had learned Morse and were deemed to have become marginally proficient, we began to listen to and copy code. Since we were to copy on typewriters, which the Army called "mills" for some reason, we also had to learn to type (now called keyboarding) with at least minimal proficiency. I'm not sure a secretarial school of the day would have awarded us certificates, but, with the use of short cuts and "field expedients," not unlike those I had used with Sister Stanislaus, we achieved acceptable competence. And we practiced and grew better. The copying and the typing were brought together, and our typing skills soon enabled us to copy faster than we could by hand. (That, after all, was the object of the exercise.) Ten words a minute, fifteen words a minute, twenty; for some reason, a memory persists that thirty words a minute was a magic number for establishing an acceptable skills level.

There is an old joke in which a New York cabbie is asked how to get to Carnegie Hall and he responds, "Practice, practice." That is what we did for most of our twenty-six weeks at Fort Devens. We practiced, every day, *ad infinitum; ad nauseum!* We began early. I remember being marched across the parade ground from the barracks to the classrooms well before dawn. In fact, I am quite sure that, at least once, I fell asleep marching to class. Certainly, I suddenly found myself several feet away from the formation of marching men, with no idea how I got there.

As with every new assignment or change of duty station, Devens confronted one with the necessity of creating a new circle of friends. We all arrived alone and few had previous friends or acquaintances in the barracks. Socialization though was probably easier there than it would normally be. The ASA School was not the place to look for heterogeneity. Not only was the intake close to lily white, but it was also highly educated – well above the norm for that day. Probably because of the AGCT testing, there was a very high ratio of college graduates as well as men who had at least a year or two of higher education. I was one of the few who had not gone beyond high school. Upon arrival, we were all socially in the same boat and the large degree of homogeneity, as well as the normal forced proximity of barracks life did make the process easier. In addition, by now we had all pretty well learned the necessity for tact and discretion in dealing with people whose bunks were, after all, only eighteen or so inches away from your own. It might here be noted that that degree of proximity, plus germ theory had persuaded the Army to adopt an alternating head to toe sleeping arrangement. On rare occasions this might lead to quite interesting discussions of personal hygiene; or the lack thereof.

As we sorted out our personal relations and preferred companions, we also began to enjoy weekend passes. Fort Devens was located in Ayer, Massachusetts, not too far from Lowell, Leominster and Fitchburg. The area then still had a significant number of factories and textile mills which employed large numbers of young women. In addition to the occasional pizza, soldiers on pass on Saturday night scouted out bars and inns and taverns and road houses which those young women frequented. With many of the girls recently out of high school, even a baby-faced seventeen-year-old (who never volunteered his age) was, at least sometimes, an acceptable companion. Most of the socialization, while sometimes more vulgar than my Aunt Anne would have preferred, was a good deal less than scandalous.

Most of us were long on boast and short on experience, and few of the girls were really prepared to flout the then accepted standards of "decency." Still, a good time seemed to have been had by all and, if young men in barracks claimed non-existent conquests, there was no one to cavil and no one to scandalize. It was, for sure, a hell of a lot better than basic training.

And then, Monday came and we were back to class and striving to improve our WPM (words per minute rate) and subject to ever more practice, practice, practice. Somewhere in that process, we began to use both ears. That is, to listen to one station, assumed to be the superior formation (Division to Regiment, Regiment to Battalion) in the right ear and the inferior formation in the left ear. (Station A transmitted; Station B then responded) The norm was to have two radio receivers, with one unit in each earpiece on the headset connected to a different station. The use of both ears would be SOP (standard operating procedure) when we were in the field. And so, we began to develop the skills we would practice in the real world. Then again, practice, practice, practice.

At various stages, particularly in the first month or two, individuals would fail to meet the required standard and would pack their duffel bags and leave. The rest of us soldiered on. When we were a few weeks from graduation, we were asked to express a preference for the theater in which we would prefer to serve after graduation. The basic choices were: the Zone of the Interior (U.S.); Asia/Pacific, probably Korea, possibly Japan; or Europe. I was one of the few who indicated Asia, partially because I had enlisted due to the Korean War and felt that I had allowed myself to be sidetracked into the ASA and, more cynically, because I told myself that if I said Asia, I would be able to say the Army, at least once, gave me my choice. The latter was not logical but I can only say that I was still seventeen. In any event, the Army did give me my choice. As our course came to an end, we were granted leave, as well as orders for our next duty station. I was to report back to Fort Devens, with orders for Camp Stoneman, California and shipment, via San Francisco, as the port of embarkation. Initial destination: Japan.

The leave passed pleasantly enough in the Bronx, Rutherford, Norwalk and a day or two in New Rochelle. On one occasion, my father and I went out for a drink. In New York State, in those days, the legal drinking age was eighteen, though virtually no bartender in any state bothered to "proof" men in uniform. Even in Massachusetts, which was a "twenty-one" state, it was not hard to get a drink at seventeen – though it was easier at upscale bars and restaurants than at the dingier ones. In any event, I offered to buy and my father ordered a scotch and soda, which probably cost thirty or thirty-five cents at that time. That sounded very adult to me so I ordered one as well. I almost immediately realized that I would never be a scotch drinker, and when he offered to buy a round, I asked for a beer. He protested because I had paid for scotch, and beer was only five or ten cents a glass. When I said I didn't like it, he suggested that if I kept on drinking it, I would acquire a taste for it. I responded, "Why should I continue to pay thirty-five cents a glass to develop a taste for something I don't like?" I still don't drink scotch – which causes some of my friends to think me a barbarian.

When we returned to Devens we had only five or six days to "clear post" and catch a train for California. To "clear post" was to gratify the Army's desire that, as you left one duty station for another, you were to leap through a number of bureaucratic hoops to prove that you were leaving no lingering problems behind. To that end, you went from office to office, collecting chits or checking boxes to prove that you were free to go; right down to establishing that you owed no books to the post library. For overseas postings, it was also necessary to inventory all issued clothing, boots, etc., to insure that you were still in possession of all uniforms and equipment which you had been issued. If not, then it would be replaced, at your expense (a "statement of charges" was issued against future pay) prior to your departure. In pursuit of these goals we spent several days going from one office to another and counting pairs of socks and boxer shorts.

It was also necessary to have your shot record form up to date. It proved you had the necessary shots for the area to which you were being sent. If you misplaced it, then you had to take all your shots over again. The night before we left, we had a farewell party (there were only about eight of us in the group) and consumed rather more alcohol than was prudent. The lack of wisdom in our conduct was forcibly brought to our attention about 0700 hours the next morning when the chapel bells across the street from our transient barracks began to peal. A peal of bells can be a joyous sound, though not when one is sound asleep and nursing a hangover. Hangover or no hangover, we awakened, shaved, had breakfast, shouldered our duffel bags and got on a bus to go to Worcester, Massachusetts where, as the Army put it, we would "entrain" for California and, ultimately Asia.

We were joined by three or four other enlisted men before we boarded the train. One of them was placed in charge of the group because he was the ranking private (E-2) by virtue of seniority of service. Collectively, we could not muster even a single PFC (E-3, private, first class). (See Appendix B.)

In addition to berths in Pullman cars, the Army had provided meal tickets for each man, entitling us to three meals a day in the dining car. The manager of the dining car interpreted this very narrowly and was prepared, begrudgingly, to allow us to order the least expensive items on the menu. One of our number, a well-to-do "imperial New Yorker," deftly dealt with our dilemma. "Nobody tips West of Buffalo," he said and instructed us that at each meal two or three of us were to prominently display a dollar bill at our place setting as we sat down. It worked. At each meal, the dining car waiters cheerfully served us whatever menu items we ordered. Similarly, when we found ourselves lacking alcoholic refreshments during a brief layover in Chicago, we made the necessary alterations in the date of birth of my baptismal certificate, which for some long-forgotten reason I had with me, and purchased liquor. We did take the precaution of sending in a soldier who physically appeared significantly older than I did.

We saw a lot of the country from our train windows and had a much clearer notion of how big it really was by the time we got to Pittsburg, California, and Camp Stoneman. We soon learned that we had just missed the sailing of a troopship and that we would be in transient status for at least a week or ten days. With memories of Camp Kilmer in mind, I told my friends that we needed to find temporary jobs quickly. They thought it unnecessary. I said, "OK, if you want to spend ten days on KP or whitewashing rocks around some Headquarters Company, be my guest." On second thought, they decided to join my search. The fact that we could all type was a valuable tool on what was essentially an administrative base. By the next morning we were assigned to a small Quartermaster operation. The work was light and simple, easily understood and not at all difficult, and we pulled no KP and painted no rocks prior to our departure. The Commanding Officer was a Major called Mullin who had been commissioned at eighteen or so, early in World War II. He treated us like old comrades and shared "old soldier's tales" with us. Indeed, the first time we saw him, our first day assigned to his office, he came in and found us drinking coffee with his NCOs and clerks. When he went to get his own coffee, he found there were no clean mugs. His response was, "What the hell kind of Army is this, everybody's drinking coffee and no cup for the God damn Major!"

One story which he shared with us went back to his earliest days as a commissioned officer. He was a 2nd Lieutenant, fresh out of OCS (Officers Candidate School), who was commanding a basic training company, in Fort Knox, KY, in a rapidly expanding Army. He was in command because his date of commissioning date was about a month earlier than the other 2nd Lieutenant assigned to the company. It probably dates from the summer of 1941. Major Mullin was a slight man, probably no more than 5'5" or 5'6" tall and then quite young. His company was comprised primarily of farmers and coal miners, most of whom were physically much larger than he. When he taught a lesson or explained a maneuver to his company, almost invariably an anonymous voice would call out, "and a little child shall lead them." He broached the problem to the First Sergeant, an old professional soldier. "Sergeant, is there any doubt in your mind as to who commands this company?"

"No, Sir."

"But there does seem to be some doubt in the minds of the troops?"

"Yes, Sir."

It was brutally hot at that point in the training cycle. Mullin ordered the company to fall out, with full field packs and overcoats at 0600 the following morning. When the company was formed, he addressed it. "We are going on a twenty mile route march, with full packs and overcoats this morning. 'And a little child shall lead them' in the back of a big ass jeep." The problem, Mullin maintained, did not recur.

The time passed relatively quickly and we soon found ourselves heading for San Francisco and the Port of Embarkation for Japan, *en route* to Korea. The ship, the *U.S.S. William Mitchell* embarked a mixed group of soldiers and airmen and set sail for the Orient. When she passed under the Golden Gate Bridge and headed out to sea, both the setting and the atmosphere were larger than life and heavy with mixed emotions. In addition to the hundreds of troops, we had also embarked a significant number of wives and other dependents on their way to Japan to join husbands and fathers who were stationed there. (There were, as yet, few women in the Army whose length of service or rank would have entitled them to dependent travel.) We were, as a result, treated to one of the lingering remnants of the old, pre-World War II Army. Each day, as meals were served, announcements rang through the ship that "Officers and their ladies and enlisted men and their wives ..." were being served. Even at seventeen it struck me as rather wonderfully archaic.

Quite quickly, large numbers of soldiers and airmen and many sailors as well, succumbed to seasickness. The ocean did not appear to be particularly turbulent, but apparently there is a peculiar chop to the waters as one departs the Northern California coast. I am not prone to motion sickness and, despite the omnipresent reek of vomit and the cacophony of retching, while queasy, I had avoided vomiting until the second day out. At that point, the sight of a very tall sailor, well over six feet, throwing up into large garbage can did me in and I too succumbed. After a day or two, most of us "got our sea legs" and life assumed a measure of normality. For a few, the nightmare of *mal de mer* would persist until the end of the voyage. We were very crowded. In the berthing areas, the bunks were very close together and tiered about four high. Those who had chosen the lowest bunk, or even the second tier, discovered during the epidemic of seasickness that vomit, falling from height onto a deck surface, will splash surprisingly high. The latrines ("heads" in the Navy) were also crowded and primitive and, worst of all, the showers produced nothing but salt water. Lathering in salt water is a virtual impossibility and even as one steps out of the shower, he is, and will remain, sticky, until a freshwater shower becomes possible. The messing facilities utilized the standard compartmentalized, metal trays, but aboard ship the tables were set breast high and troops discovered that they were to eat standing up, which I am sure was intended as a device to feed the greatest number of people in the shortest amount of time. We quickly came to envy the "officers and their ladies" (and even the "enlisted men and their wives"), who dined several decks above us in far more civilized circumstances. There was little to do during the voyage but there was a small ship's library and I read most of the histories of medieval England written by Thomas Costain, a then very prominent historical novelist and popular historian. Among others, I enjoyed *The Magnificent Century* (13th) and *The Last Plantagenets*. During the voyage, on July 17, 1953, we crossed the 180th meridian, the International Date Line. While the occasion is not as storied in naval myth as crossing the equator, it was still considered a major event and we were all enrolled as members of the **Domain of the Golden Dragon.** We also "gained" a day as we crossed the Date Line. (When Pearl Harbor was attacked it was Dec. 7, 1941; when the Americans in the Philippine Islands were attacked, on the far side of the IDL, it was Dec. 8th.)

About ten or eleven days after sailing, we sailed into the harbor at Yokohama, Japan. Those of us destined for duty with the ASA, Korea, were scheduled to fly out shortly after our arrival. Prior to that, it was necessary for us to turn in all our uniforms, because duty in Korea would require only fatigue uniforms and combat boots, no Class A or B uniforms or low quarter shoes.

In the event, there would be no flight. In a very short period of time, just prior to our arrival, the Air Force had lost two troop carrier planes of different models, and all flights were grounded while an investigation was carried out. As a result, we had to wait while shipping was found to transport us to Korea by sea. We thus had an opportunity to explore Japan, or at least the Tokyo/ Yokohama area, though little of what we did was culturally or intellectually uplifting. We had time on our hands and we tended to drift, mostly in a group of about six or seven and mostly from bar to bar. On one occasion, I think as a result of a cabdriver misreading the situation, we ended up in a bordello. As world-weary sophisticates (aged seventeen to about twenty-two) we did not wish to be considered country bumpkins, so we settled down and ordered beers. Along with the beer, an appropriate number of young women also arrived. Some conversation ensued, made awkward by the language problem as well as the situation in which we found ourselves. We had not intended to end up in a brothel. We were there for about an hour or an hour and a half during which about half of us "went upstairs." The remaining half had more beers and tried to explain, somewhat red-facedly, that we could not "go upstairs" because General MacArthur (whose name was revered in Japan) would not approve. How we got around the fact that President Truman had removed MacArthur from command in 1951, I no longer remember; perhaps we just didn't care. I think we really wanted to explore the possibilities, but some combination of religion and thoughts of our mothers and equally significant though more pedestrian ideals and mores prevailed. As a sidebar, two of the "girls" claimed to be "Hiroshima Maidens," a collective term given to female survivors of the Atomic Bombing of Hiroshima and Nagasaki. Certainly both of them had significant burn scarring. Of course, since most of Japan had been fire bombed for months prior to war's end, burn scars were not rare. Being a "Hiroshima Maiden" though, probably brought bigger tips. Once the group was reunited, we, especially those who had remained downstairs, quite sheepishly, returned to post. Informed that we would sail for Korea from the former Japanese naval base at Sasebo on July 28th, we completed our preparations. The night before, on July 27th, the truce was signed, ending the Korean War. The party that night was an excellent one, though, for reasons I have never satisfactorily understood, it seemed to me more somber than jubilant. Anyway, we were off for Korea, "the Land of the Morning Calm."

We arrived in the Korean harbor of Pusan and entrained. Our next stop was scheduled at a replacement depot from which individual soldiers would be allotted to the units in which they were to serve. The railroad station gave most of us our first sense of war. Pusan had been the linchpin of the defense of South Korea in mid-1950. The Republic of Korea troops (ROK) and U.S. troops had rallied at Pusan, establishing the "Pusan Perimeter," and holding off the North Korean invasion while awaiting the arrival of reinforcements from the U.S. Then, in September, when the U.S. First Marine Division's Inchon landings restored mobility to the battlefield, the American Eighth Army broke out and drove north. The Pusan region, as a result, had suffered great destruction. The physical devastation we saw shocked us, though Seoul seemed much worse. My first thoughts when I saw Pusan, and particularly, the Capital, Seoul, was the newsreel photographs of Berlin in 1945. One did not see structures, but the skeletons of structures. In the railroad depot at Pusan, however, the shock was less the physical devastation, than the children. They haunted the tracks around the station. Each of us had been given an issue of C Rations for the trip north. One component of the C Ration was two hard crackers. The lineal descendants of the hardtack of the navies of the 18th and 19th centuries, and of Civil War armies, these had changed little since the days when troops broke the crackers with their rifle butts and sopped them in bacon grease to try to make them edible. We, spoiled as we were, just threw them out the train windows. The train was not moving but, even so, the way the Korean children threw themselves under the train to grab those crackers allowed me, for the first time, to really know what it meant to be hungry. I have never forgotten one boy, perhaps eight or nine years old. He had lost one leg just above the knee and the foot on the other leg just forward of the ankle. He moved using his butt, his one heel and his hands with a wonderful, if pitiable, dexterity. I am happy to say that, without a word being said, most of us just tossed the rest of our rations, or most of the remainder, out the windows for the kids. "And I learned about life from them."

A short time after we reached the replacement depot, the ASA contingent was trucked, "embussed," to our Headquarters, the 501st Group in Seoul and there allotted to individual units. I was assigned to the 326th Communications Reconnaissance Company. Those of us bound for the 326th once again climbed on trucks, this time headed north out of Seoul on MSR (Main Supply Route) 3A, headed toward Uijongbu. In perhaps thirty or forty minutes, we arrived at the compound of the 326th, a single company post. It was on low ground, surrounded by ridges and heights, a genuinely picturesque setting, and completely enfolded in the less than aromatic miasma of rice paddies. Korean rice paddies, at least in 1953 and 1954, were regularly fertilized with human ordure. In the heat of late July and early August, we quickly realized that we would be making significant adjustments. We got off the trucks in front of Company Headquarters (HQ) and were told that the Company Commander (Commanding Officer/CO) would soon be out to address us.

As we waited, another adjustment was made clear to us. MSR 3A was largely a dirt road, with occasional paving, disturbed by three years of military traffic. It had, necessarily, been a bumpy ride. It was not long after we arrived that voices began asking directions to the nearest latrine. The response was unexpected. A yard or so away from the HQ building, there was a flimsy, wood and canvas structure perhaps 40" high, 2' wide and 2' deep, forming a canvas rectangle, open on one side. In the center, dug into the ground at a slight angle was a hollow cylinder about twice the diameter of a drain pipe. This was a classic example of what the Army refers to as a "field expedient." That is a thing to be used when the actual item is unavailable. It was, rather inelegantly, referred to as a "piss tube." Since this was located less than ten yards off the road, and due to the fact that there was a nearby Korean village, and female Koreans were passing by virtually constantly, this set up a genuine cultural challenge. Some time passed before, metaphorically, the dam broke and another adjustment was accepted, though never welcomed. I should probably mention here that in the characteristically casual practice of that day, the women (formally "indigenous population" or "indigenous personnel") were always spoken of as "mama-sans." Male adults were "papa-sans." Koreans and other Asians were also usually, if not always, referred to as "gooks." Regrettably, I do not recall anyone of us, ever, suggesting there was anything wrong with that.

While we had traveled north from Pusan, we had seen trainloads of North Korean and Chinese Prisoners of War *en route* home pursuant to the terms of the truce. The repatriation of POWs had been one of the sticking points in the prolonged truce negotiations. The South Koreans and the Americans had opposed the forcible repatriation of those prisoners who did not wish to be returned. In mid-June, 1953, just about a month prior to the armistice, South Korea's President, Syngman Rhee released somewhere around 25,000 of about 35,000 North Korean prisoners. Ostensibly, they were those who wanted to stay in South Korea. Although this was disturbing to American negotiators, it rapidly became clear that the Chinese delegates only cared about Chinese repatriation, and in July the truce agreement was concluded. Still, at the time of our arrival, U.S. military posts, or at least isolated ones like ours, were agitated about the possibility of enemies at large. As a result, when we arrived and for some little time after, the troops kept their weapons in their tents, more or less at the ready. It was as close to the war as we were ever to come.

After the CO had addressed us, largely to inform us of his expectations as to our behavior, we were allotted to our platoons and duty stations and to the tents which, winter and summer, were our quarters. We lived in what were known as "squad tents," which in a pinch could hold about a dozen men in reasonable comfort but which, in practice usually held about eight or ten. They were 16' x 32' and could easily encompass three or four cots down each 32' side and one to each side of the door frame on the 16' sides.

In the summer, when we arrived, in pleasant weather, the canvas sides rolled up for "air conditioning" which allowed the troops to benefit from any air moving. Of course, if the breeze was coming off the rice paddies, it provided "air with body to it," as we said at the time. In the summer, since Korea was malarial, we slept beneath frames of mosquito netting, which tended to block at least portions of the breeze, though not the odors. We were also required to take prophylactic anti-malarial tablets once a week. You got the pill, I think on Sunday in the Mess Hall, took it in front of a clerk, and then went into the chow line. No pill, no food, plus a visit with one officer or another.

In winter the tents were heated by two oil burning stoves set on a center line equidistant from the two doors. The oil flowed through narrow hoses, gravity-fed from 55 gallon drums of oil, set on frames outside the tent. When the oil ran out, the drum was replaced. Since there were no gauges, you only knew the drum had run dry when you woke up with water frozen in your wash basins or canteen cups, a not infrequent occurrence. The tent's water supply was carried, in five gallon jerry cans from the company water point; a medium sized water trailer which was brought to the compound from a quartermaster station. Light was provided by electrical wiring extending the length of the tent at the roof peak. Two flexes descended from the central source, roughly at one-third intervals. Below the lights, were wooden frames, crude "tables" with appropriate sized holes to hold the wash basins we used for shaving and washing. A separate building was provided for communal showers.

We slept on folding canvas cots with bed linens and blankets during much of the year. Due to the cold of Korean winters though, we then slept in excellent winter weight sleeping bags. Due to their shape and the way the sleeper's head and shoulders were framed within the bag, we called them "mummy bags." We also had heavier weight winter uniforms, already in Army green, as well as caps with earlaps. Our field jackets had liners that buttoned or zipped into them. We were also provided with galoshes, shoe pacs (boots with felt liners) or what were then called "Mickey Mouse" boots, an early example of thermal footwear. While on guard duty, for example, in winter cold, one was cold but not dangerously so. While these conditions were relatively primitive, in many other ways we were highly pampered. Each tent, for example, had a "houseboy." Usually a teenaged Korean, the houseboy made our beds, swept and mopped the floors, took our soiled clothing to the local "mama-san," who was a laundress, toted in the water supply and otherwise was at our beck and call. Due the availability of "indigenous personnel" to perform virtually all menial chores, we were also free from KP and any sort of beautification of the post which might occur to the CO. I do not any longer remember what all of this cost, but it was certainly marginal, that is, measured in dollars rather than tens of dollars. At that point, PFCs received about $115.00 a month.

In more than one case, our houseboys were displaying the entrepreneurial spirit which would stand South Korea in good stead in its later development. In my tent, the houseboy was named Kim. That name was so common in Korea that it was subject to rather stereotypical usage, but in this case, I do believe it was his name.

I should here note that U.S. currency was not distributed to American troops in Korea. We were paid in MPC, Military Payment Certificates, which could be called in at any moment and replaced with another issue, leaving those holding the old certificates with worthless paper. Short form: one bright morning, a formation was held and troops were informed that the new MPC were to be distributed. You got your wallet or stash or whatever, went to the appropriate line and handed in your MPC and received the same amount in the newly issued MPCs. The idea was, I think, to avoid counterfeiting, and currency manipulation and difficulty with the domestic economy. If one was involved in the black market, a recall of MPC was a genuine fear. An unwitting Korean who had black market dealings could wake up with thousands of dollars in MPC and go to bed broke, with lots of handsomely engraved paper of no monetary value.

To tell this story, I begin with the arrival of a large package of tea bags from my Aunt Anne who knew that, at least occasionally, I drank tea. The box was kept on a shelf above my cot along with various other items, shaving gear, and so on. One lazy day, I decided to have a cup of tea and reached for the box. As I went to take out a tea bag, I noticed that the box seemed needlessly heavy and I removed a layer or two of tea. When "what to my wondering eyes should appear" but a wad of MPC large enough to choke "the proverbial horse." It contained well over $1500.00. Several of us speculated briefly, but there was no rational explanation other than that my box of tea was where Kim kept his stash from black market operations. I liked Kim and I was not particularly disturbed about the black market; Koreans were just keeping body and soul together. Indeed, if you simply looked around, you would often see small, hovel-like, houses, shining brightly in the sun. The sparkling reflection was due to the fact that the siding was often weatherproofed with abandoned, flattened beer cans, available courtesy of the U.S. Army. Anyway, I showed Kim the stash, which surely did not surprise him, and told him that since it might implicate me, he was never to keep it in or around my bunk area and wrote it off as a story to tell my grandchildren. While I was "in country," there was one general recall and reissue of MPC and my memory is of Koreans besieging us through the gates and through the barbed wire around the compound looking for soldiers to accept and exchange the currency for them, at almost any premium. I don't recall many takers, but then public acceptance would not have been a good idea anyway. Quite aside from ethical concerns, a low ranking enlisted man (EM) exchanging a large amount of money would certainly have raised significant questions.

We did have a mess hall, a prefabricated structure in which our meals were prepared and served, our cooks and bakers generously supplemented by "indigenous personnel"; we even had a non-commissioned officers club in a Quonset hut. Back home, only non-commissioned officers were allowed in NCO Clubs. In Korea, or at least in the 326th, all EM were welcome. The club, in a peculiar way, became a way to assess the post-war atmosphere versus the wartime atmosphere. About a month after my arrival, there was a Korea-wide "flap." It seems that the then still politically potent **Women's Christian Temperance Union** had become aware that soldiers under twenty-one years of age were being allowed to drink alcohol in NCO clubs. What might have been prudently overlooked in war was intolerable in peace. The Army, in its awesome majesty, responded quickly. All NCO club cards were called in and new cards issued. For troops under twenty-one, the new cards were stamped **Minor Under Twenty One**. (I still have mine.) I assume the **WCTU** was happy and, since the stamp had no effect whatsoever on who was served alcohol, the troops were indifferent. Tact, discretion and a blind eye operated, as they so often do as a social emollient.

Work areas, times and functions were abnormally rigidly divided. First, there was a large sort of "public" area of the post where we all lived and messed and where some EM carried out their duties. For example, cooks and bakers, armorers and mechanics, the company clerical personnel and so on. Then, there was an inner compound, reached through a sort of guard shack/ switchboard, manned by an armed operator, twenty-four hours a day. It was in that compound that intercept operators, traffic analysts and cryptanalysts carried on the work which formed the *raison d'etre* of the company. Their working day was twenty-four hours, divided into three shifts or "tricks." In brief, a platoon or more of men were occupied in intercepting the communications of the People's Volunteer Army (the Red Chinese Army) and subjecting it to analysis from 0700 until 1500; another group relieved them at 1500 and was itself relieved at 2300. That final group then pursued its duties until 0700. Every third week, if memory serves, we got a full day and a half or two days off. No one who did not possess a top secret security clearance was allowed entry to the security area. There was virtually no social intermingling between troops who worked in the security area and those who worked outside it.

Each platoon had thirty to forty intercept operators. All inhabitants of an individual tent worked the same "trick." As a result, we worked together, we ate together, we slept together and we amused one another. We also drank together. Proximity and shared interests (at least professionally) tended to transition into genuine closeness, and the largest portion of us came to genuinely like one another. Once again, as at Fort Devens, most of the men I worked with were college graduates. By and large, we pretty well covered the country geographically. I have particular memories of men from New York City, from the Philadelphia area, from Massachusetts and from California. There were few Southerners as I recall, though I remember one ROTC Lieutenant from Texas, and a highly energetic and colorful lad from Picayune, Mississippi. I can think of only one man of color, he was from St. Louis. Others came from Minnesota and Michigan, The group with which I had the greatest affinity was essentially urban and, mostly, Northeastern. Still, there was a general level of collegiality with most of my comrades. We were all young, generally well educated, Caucasian, Christian, with a slight sprinkling of Jews, and city-bred.

We were restricted, for the most part, to a small piece of ground, surrounded on three sides by rice paddies and on the fourth by MSR-3A. Of necessity, we bonded. First, we exchanged stories and backgrounds. In the course of those initial conversations, I had another, genuine, "small world" experience. As it turned out, Dave McCourt was a graduate of Manhattan College and, in the course of a conversation, it turned out that a pledge to Dave's fraternity had brought my cousin Judith as his date to a fraternity function where she and Dave had met. She was a pretty girl which was probably why he remembered her. Dave, like most of the group, had a quick and, on occasion devastating, wit. Jack Gordon, who grew up in the Philadelphia suburbs, was charming, and even faster with a quip than Dave and was a clotheshorse to boot. You could hand Jack a pair of fatigues right off a quartermaster shelf, with the tags still hanging on them and, when he put them on, they looked tailor-made. Marty Malone, our Californian, was somewhat quieter but, when the mood was on him, no less devastating verbally. Roger Breakey, from Massachusetts, somehow seemed slightly older, though no slower, than the rest (though they all were between twenty-two and twenty-five). He was a superb storyteller. In addition to being, or seeming to me to be, paragons of wit and of sarcasm, they also had depth – which sometimes surfaced in startling ways. Roger and Marty and I were tent mates. One evening, Marty was quietly reading *The Imitation of Christ,* when he suddenly reared up on his cot, threw the book across the tent and shouted something like, "The only way I could do this would be to slash my wrists." I suspect that was not why the book was written. It was a rather daunting group for an about to be eighteen-year old to enter. Over the next year or so I would learn a great deal about how to tell a story, to make or illustrate a point, the utility of *repartee* and the impact of humor from all of them. I also was continually being presented with tidbits from the Western cultural canon (e.g. *The Imitation of Christ)*, though I was not conscious of it.

Our usual day, regardless of what "trick" we were pulling, involved reporting to our work stations in the security area and taking over from the previous operators. If the network for which we were responsible was "up," that is, transmitting, we tried to move into position and begin copying as seamlessly as possible. The usual form was to have the network control, for purposes of illustration, perhaps an infantry regiment, in our right ear, and the "outstations," perhaps battalions, in our left ear. Thus, the 212th Regiment would "call" its First Battalion and indicate that it had "traffic." That is, that there were messages to be sent and received. The battalion would acknowledge, and traffic would be sent. The radio receivers were located at the intercept operator's left shoulder and immediately in front of him was a mill (typewriter). Threaded into the mill was a roll of paper, four or five sheets in thickness, with carbon paper between each page (not unlike a roll of wrapping paper in an old fashioned store). Each page was a different color: one color destined, e.g., for traffic analysis, another for cryptanalysis, etc. The operator indicated   which station he was copying and copied the messages and responses until the transmission was completed. The quality of the copy was dependent upon atmospheric conditions (the presence or absence of static), the intercept operator's own competence, the condition of the radio equipment and the skills of the transmitting operator.

Every Morse operator has a distinctive way of transmitting, a signature as it were, which is called a "fist." A competent intercept operator was usually able to identify one of his usual contacts by the sound of his "fist." As a general rule, Chinese operators were well trained and their transmissions were characterized by smoothness and clarity. After the 212th had finished with its First Battalion, it might contact another battalion, or a logistical formation or a higher headquarters, but the process remained the same. When we arrived, the various units and formations, their relationships, locales and radio frequencies (the network), were all known quantities. In addition to the analyses which I have already mentioned, once you knew the frequency upon which a unit broadcast, it was a relatively simple matter to arrange for three stations to copy a unit at the same time. Using radio direction finding triangulation, you could then nail its geographic location. In simple form, on or about August 1, 1953, we knew which outfits we were copying, what call signs they used, where they were and what frequencies each of them broadcast on. During my sixteen months in Korea, there was only one major signals upheaval: when all units of the PVA simultaneously changed all call signs and all broadcasting frequencies.

The result was an absolute zoo. Suddenly, we had nothing and had very little to go on. A major tool in the search was the "ear" of experienced intercept operators. That meant that each operator was given a range of likely frequencies for an aural search. The expectation was that at least some of us would hear something which would enable us to identify some unit of the PVA by ear. That is, to identify by recognition of the "fist" of one or more Chinese operators. During this quite unusually exciting and frantically busy time, a number of men, probably ten or more years older than we, appeared, dressed in fatigues, though with no sign of rank or military identification. We, for example, wore the patch of the Eighth Army's First Corps. They kept to themselves and never mingled with us, but we believed that they were the sources of useful information, such as which frequencies might profitably be probed. I now believe that they were experienced operatives of the National Security Agency. At that time, I'm not even sure that I knew such an agency existed.

In any event, it was a period of extraordinary activity. Memory suggests that near normality was restored within a two or three week period. Changing technology has made it all moot now, but the Chinese would probably have achieved better results if they had transferred operators between units at the same time they changed call signs and frequencies. Once we had reestablished contact with the units for which we were responsible, often by recognizing one or more "fists," we returned, again, to a more featureless world, with one day very like another.

While much of our daily existence revolved around our radios, in a few ways we still functioned as soldiers. While most ancillary functions: KP, garbage details, etc., were now carried on by indigenous personnel (Koreans), we still, for instance, "pulled guard duty." Each day, from shortly before sunset until just after dawn, troops, in addition to their prescribed duties, also guarded the compound as a whole, and provided additional guards within the secure areas. All who appeared were challenged and required to demonstrate their right to be within the area. This was one of the few areas in which officers assigned to the 326th found themselves pursuing a traditional role. Our lieutenants had been peripherally exposed to the functions of the company but had not been trained in any of our duties. Thus, other than in irregular inspections and/or our almost miniscule responsibilities in relation to the motor pool, they had little contact with us and few or no responsibilities in relation to the performance of our duties. We did also, once or twice a year, find ourselves being trucked out to a rifle range so that we could undergo weapons qualification. Once again, here our officers had a genuine role. Otherwise, it must have been a deadly dull assignment with, at best, only a highly limited role to play in the company's function and few opportunities to exercise professional leadership.

As a result, when seeming opportunities presented themselves, there was on occasion a tendency to overreact. An illustration: I was Sergeant of the Guard on a given evening and, according to custom, prior the posting of the guard, there had been an inspection of the guards (Guard Mount). The OD (Officer of the Day), an ROTC commissioned lieutenant from Texas, and I inspected the troops. As we inspected one trooper, he ordered me to "gig" the soldier in question because he needed a haircut. Which he did. I said to the Lieutenant, "Sir, there has not been a barber available on post for more than two weeks." I was, again, ordered to mark him as deficient. I did so. A gig could bring disciplinary action against a soldier at the company commander's discretion. Later that evening, Lieutenant Blank, as he was called (the OD), was preparing for sleep when he realized that his tent mate (officers usually were only two to a tent) was out on a truck convoy and it was not clear when he would return. The lieutenant knew he would have difficulty sleeping with the unshaded light bulbs hanging from the tent's power line, so he decided to "solve" his dilemma by wrapping a towel around the light bulb to reduce the glare, and went to sleep. Inevitably, the towel caught fire. The closest guard, sighting the fire, shouted, "Fire." As Sergeant of the Guard (and not sleeping) I turned out the guard, the firefighters came out and the small blaze was quickly extinguished. There was minimal damage.

One of my duties as Sergeant of the Guard was to write up the guard book, a sort of diary of the activities covered by that time period. I wrote something like, "Lieutenant Blank wrapped a towel around a light bulb. The light bulb caught fire. Guard turned out and fire extinguished." When the lieutenant arrived at the conclusion of the shift, I presented the guard book for his signature, which was required. He said he couldn't sign that. I said, "Is there anything there which did not occur?" He agreed there was not. I then said that if he couldn't sign it, I would have to take it to the CO and ask him what the next step should be. He signed the book. I felt marginally guilty; I could have softened it. The "gigged" soldier, on the other hand, felt much better about the world.

On another occasion, having been found wanting during a tent inspection, by a different officer, whom we will call Lieutenant Sloper, two of us were ordered, in our free time, to paint the security shack. That was the partial Quonset hut, functioning as a security checkpoint and switchboard, through which we entered the secure compound. For some reason, the top had a very large canvas cover tautly drawn over it. Upon asking, we were informed by Sloper that the canvas, too, should be painted. We requisitioned paint and spray guns and checked a 2 and 1/2 ton truck out of the motor pool to provide pressure for the spray gun. Perched at the peak of the roof's curve, we were astonished by the amount of paint which the canvas absorbed, with no noticeable change in color or texture. At best, in fifteen or twenty minutes, we had a discernable impact on no more than a square foot. By now, both fascinated and amused, we remained obedient to the letter of our orders, continuing the task for a couple of hours and using up an awful lot of paint. Lt. Sloper did not appear during this time, so we stayed hard at it though we did from time to time ask each other if we should speak to the lieutenant. Then we would laugh and apply more paint. When he finally appeared, he castigated us for not working, but we offered to provide witnesses to our diligence: the security shack was one of the most public places in the compound, and we showed him ten or more empty paint cans. The latter appeared to take him aback. After walking around for a few moments, he concluded that we had been adequately disciplined and dismissed us. We did not laugh until we were out of sight; though, in the months that followed, we would, going in and out of the security shack, occasionally look, with amusement, at the canvas on the roof and the odd discoloration around the top of the Quonset.

In the British Army, prior to World War II, they still had on the books an offense known as "dumb insolence," which might have applied in this instance. Lieutenant Sloper and his friend, called Lieutenant Jones, were, in fact, known to the enlisted men in a term of both pity and scorn, as "helpless and hopeless." In a unit where they had an opportunity to actually work with their men, there might have been some room for development for them. In the 326th, they were "just spinning their wheels."

Lt. Jones was the motor pool officer when I arrived at the unit. We were equipped for mobile operation, with a substantial number of what were called "hut trucks." These were 2 ½ ton trucks ("deuce and a halfs") with structures on the back which contained radio equipment so that, if necessary, operators could be moved forward to intercept signals which were, perhaps, too weak to be picked up by our antenna array and for various other purposes. Most of us were assigned as drivers to some vehicle from the motor pool. When I was assigned to drive a deuce and a half, I informed the motor sergeant and through him, Lt. Jones, that I did not know how to drive. Lt. Jones instructed the motor sergeant to give me a written driver's test. I assume he thought that I was lying to avoid duties in the motor pool. I failed the test, though, to my surprise, not terribly badly. I don't know if the Lieutenant thought I was still faking or what, but he instructed the motor sergeant to issue me a license anyway. Faced with a *fait accompli,* I asked my friend, a fellow called Lee, from Pennsylvania, to give me a couple of quick lessons. Most of the vehicles were still "standard shift," though a few of the hut trucks had automatic transmission. Motor pool duty was not very onerous. Motor pool mechanics kept the vehicles running and, primarily, what we did was to take our trucks down to the river once a week and give some Korean kids a few packs of cigarettes to wash the trucks, then drive them back and park them. All went well for a month or so. Then, the odds caught up with me (so did being eighteen). As I was returning the truck, I got a littler fancier than my skill set could handle and caught the bumper of my truck on the bumper of another truck. Lt. Jones was livid and announced that he would be preparing a "statement of charges," requiring me to reimburse the army for the cost of the accident. I then requested a meeting in which I reminded him that I had made clear that I did not know how to drive; that I had failed the written test and that he had insisted that I be issued a license anyway. I was removed from the motor pool duty roster and never heard anything more about the incident or about the statement of charges.

There were other incidents, some individual and some institutional, which marked or punctuated my time in the "Land of the Morning Calm." One of my good friends, Lee, who had given me those driving lessons, was a fellow 1717. He discovered, after we reached Korea, that he did not like being a high speed Morse Code intercept operator. At that time we understood that our individual training cost about $10,000.00, which, in 1953-54, was a lot of money. Still, Lee chose to opt out. In effect, he became a military entrepreneur; he made himself, effectively, a permanent guard. Many guys really hated guard duty. The hours were lousy: several two-hour shifts during the course of the night; it was often too cold, or too hot; it rained, or snowed and, on occasion, things, animals, shadows and strange noises really did, in the words of the old Scot's Presbyterian prayer, "go boomp in the night." Few admitted they were frightened, but many were happy to let somebody else pull their duty. Lee's deal worked as follows. If his trick was working when you wanted him to pull your guard you had to cover his station. Then, you paid him. I think it was either $5.00 or $10.00 a night. Financially, he told me, he was making Master Sergeant's pay when he was PFC. In 1953-54, a PFC made about $115.00 a month, a Master Sergeant about $225.00. Since he was an avid gun collector, this enabled him, via mail, to order weapons, usually of historical interest, for his collection. Even that amount of money was sometimes inadequate, and I was always prepared, around payday, to hand over $25.00 to $50.00 in MPC for a pending purchase. This was a matter of a convenient arrangement between friends, and interest was not an issue. Repayment was prompt. There was, after all, no place other than the NCO Club to spend money, and drinks there were never more than 25cents, and beer only a dime. Cigarettes, my pursuing vice, were $1.10 a carton for *Pall Malls.* Unlike most soldiers, Lee was able to have the army allow him to serve ***his way***.

He was also central to a very interesting adventure/misadventure just before Christmas, 1953. In addition to the physical destruction of the war, the movement of troops and the disruption of civil society had also spawned armies of prostitutes. Seoul was a hotbed of brothels and *bagnios.* It was also a vast open air flea market, with hundreds of items for sale, ranging from stolen fatigue uniforms to the crude wash basins we used in our tents, to various curios. Among the latter were some really well-made and even artistic letter openers, made and decorated as miniature *samurai* swords. Lee had decided that he would purchase a number of the letter openers as Christmas presents for his family back in Pennsylvania.

He hitched a ride on a truck heading into Seoul and began a search. Of course, he spoke no Korean and the Koreans to whom he spoke made certain assumptions and had agendas of their own. Armored in innocence and virtue (he was after all in quest of Christmas presents) and trusting in the assurance that he was being brought to a source for the merchandise he sought, he followed the leader. As he told me the story, he ended up in a whorehouse where his repeated requests for samurai sword letter openers fell upon deaf ears. Next, his own ears picked up the sound of two-way radios as the U.S. Military Police began a raid on the house. I should note here that the Army punished soldiers patronizing such houses severely. The Army was less driven by moral tenets than by the medical costs and loss of duty hours which resulted from venereal disease. Lee was suddenly and unceremoniously shoved into a closet/secret room, behind some sort of sliding panel and left to his own devices. He spent the next hour or so in hiding, hoping that the MPs who were thoroughly searching, would not find him. After the raid, he was rather unceremoniously tossed out and somewhat sheepishly and with difficulty found his way back to central Seoul and thence to the 326th. When he told me the story, his last words on the whole saga were, "and, Tom, I still don't have any letter openers."

Christmas naturally causes me to think of religious affairs and events, and there are a few interesting moments regarding religion and distinguished visitors, which I might summarize as involving ***the pastor and the priests*** and ***prelate and pulchritude.*** As a single company post, we were not entitled to have an Army chaplain assigned to us, and, indeed, we rarely saw a Catholic chaplain under any circumstances. Catholic services were available each Sunday, courtesy of the Columban Fathers. They were a missionary order which, primarily composed of Irish priests, with a smattering of Americans, had found their duty in Korea for many years. In any event, each Sunday, one of them, stationed in the area, would swing by and say Mass for the RCs among us. There was no regularity, so, to my knowledge, none of us got to know any of them other than as "ships that pass in the night." There was an Army chaplain, whom we shall call Major Travers, who was assigned to the 501st Group. We saw Major Travers at least once a month when he would arrive at the post for a Troop Information and Education session. By denomination and nativity, he was a Southern Baptist and a virtual caricature of the more annoying stereotypes that brings to mind. Among other things, he had a disdain for Catholicism which he made not the slightest effort to disguise. It was so evident in every session, that even "fallen away" Catholics were offended. Mostly, of course, in the good old Army way, troops just scurried, with or without excuses, to avoid his sessions. If inescapably cornered, one just hunkered down and tuned him out as much as possible. We did, at one point, hear a rumor that he had been caught in an MP dragnet in a "house of ill fame" in Seoul, though I cannot say that was confirmed. It did bring about a certain amount of glee, which certainly was in bad taste.

One of our genuinely decent acts as a collective, was the adoption of a Salvation Army orphanage. It is no more than a truism to say that wars create orphans. The Korean War was no exception. I don't remember how, but at some time we became aware of a nearby orphanage operated by the Salvation Army. In a short period of time, we had, as Americans do, created a committee, drawn up by-laws and elected officers. At one point, I served as Treasurer, if memory serves. We had also begun fundraising. Since the Army paid its members monthly in a pay call formation, we were benefited by the fact that we knew when everyone got paid and could swoop down on everyone at a time when it was very difficult to substantiate a claim of being broke. We could also access the Post Exchange (PX) a sort of big box store where we could get things (soap and cleaning products, e.g.) at discounted prices and then take them to the orphanage. That did necessitate a trip into Seoul, as we had no real PX facility on our small camp. I think we made the trip to see the kids about twice a month with foodstuffs, candy and cleaning paraphernalia. It was rather a return to something approaching normality, and it reinforced our motivation when we actually saw the kids.

There were two highly distinguished (though in very different ways) visitors who came to Korea during my time there. Cardinal Spellman, then certainly the best-known Catholic prelate in America, made annual pre-Christmas visits to Korea in the early 1950s and 1953 was no different. There was to be an outdoor Mass celebrated in a stadium in Seoul. I remember being asked by one of my Protestant friends whether or not I was going. I said, no. He then asked why not. I responded seriously, if somewhat flippantly that it was a damn cold day for a ride in a deuce and a half, to sit in a large stadium (also cold) in order to watch the Mass which, unless one was unusually lucky, you would need binoculars to view. Besides, I said, one of the Irish priests will be here tomorrow to say Mass, and it's the same thing. I would not physically see the Cardinal until five years later.

About two months after the Cardinal's visit, we were informed that Miss Marilyn Monroe, then visiting Japan during her honeymoon with Joe DiMaggio, was going to come to Korea, briefly, to entertain the troops. A similar conversation ensued, during which I again made reference to the cold, the discomfort of riding in the back of a truck and the viewing distance likely to prevail – which, because more people wanted to see Marilyn than the Cardinal, was likely to be even greater. I never mourned the opportunity, since I had always thought her charms somewhat overrated and my physical comfort and convenience more important. Had it been a "real girl."….

My religious experience in Korea also included my first separation from regular and consistent religious practice. I was religiously, for the first time, totally independent and that independence exhibited itself in a drifting away from regular religious observance. I suppose that I did not so much rebel against religion as I fell into some form of indifference. The effect was the same. I did go to Mass, if irregularly, though I rarely gave any thought to religion in any meaningful sense. I suppose I might draft the indifference as a bell curve which accelerated from its base, reached an apex and then began to curve back toward the base as time passed, and I decided that I was destined to be religious at some core level and began a return to my former practice. I did learn how easy it is for a young person to "rebel" against God, or organized religion, since neither responds to the rebellion in any visible way. For some, like me, the moment represents an aberration; for others, a new and profoundly different chapter in their lives. Since I would spend all of my adult, professional life with young people, many rather adrift, that knowledge was not without value.

A normal feature of a sixteen-month-tour in Korea was two trips to Japan on Rest and Recuperation (R & R) leaves of seven days each, not charged against normal leave (30 days a year leave time). These were often colloquially spoken of by the troops as I and I (Intercourse and Intoxication).

They usually stretched to ten or eleven days because of the travel time from Korea to Japan, even by plane. My first R & R, which I spent in Tokyo, was a delight. I discovered that at the main NCO Club in Tokyo, for about $1.25, one could get a filet mignon, with shrimp cocktail and all the trimmings: "from soup to nuts." I think we did that twice. I went shopping on the Ginza and discovered that at the then current rate of exchange, 360 yen to the dollar, native products of good quality were very inexpensive. I purchased a small tea set for an elderly "courtesy cousin," named Katie, as well as a variety of other small gifts. Katie was delighted with her tea set and displayed it prominently. What I did not know was that she had carefully instructed her relatives that, at her death (she was then ninety), it was to be returned to me. It sits today atop a bookcase in our living room.

I now wish that I had seized the opportunity to travel to Kyoto, the old cultural capital of Japan and to Kamakura to see the Great Buddha – but I was just eighteen and the bright lights of the big city beckoned. My friends and I did a lot of bar hopping, indulged ourselves in gracious living and thoroughly enjoyed ourselves. We did both rest and relax. We also certainly approached, perhaps even collided with, intoxication. Traditional morality, religion, military discipline, fear of venereal disease and a certain amount of timidity precluded any fulfillment of the first I. As it turned out, there was never to be a second trip to Japan. About the time that I became eligible for my second R & R, the CO decided that troops could not be spared for ten or eleven days at a time and, therefore, members of the 326th would have to take R & R "in Country." That meant that you got seven days off in Korea – but there was nowhere to go to recreate, other than maybe Seoul. Disappointed but rather philosophical, "the Army is the Army," I decided to make the best of it. I have already noted that when we arrived, I had noticed that the encampment was surrounded by some lovely country. Each day, I slept as late as I could, breakfasted, got some sandwiches from the mess hall and went hiking on the ridge lines around the post. Each day brought new vistas. One day, for example, I came upon a small, isolated, religious shrine, presumably

Buddhist, which exuded a welcome atmosphere of calm and contemplation. Many views were at least vaguely reminiscent of my beloved New York Adirondacks and that pleased me.

Returning to camp for evening chow, I would shower away the sweat of the day, read a bit and adjourn to the NCO club where the company was familiar and the drinks even cheaper than in Tokyo. I did feel cheated out of the extra two or three days, but not enough to lose any sleep. When the seven days ended, I went back to work.

"Green Eggs and Liver"

In what I remember as a single, theater-wide instance, one anomaly seemed to include all of Korea. In this instance, the Quartermaster Corps, which was responsible for all supplies provided to the entire Army in Korea, seemed to either have lost its mind or gone on vacation. For an extended period of time (it seemed like forever but was probably no more than three to five days) the only meat available for supper in the mess halls (and not just ours) was liver.

For a few troopers that was OK. For the bulk (perhaps 80% or more) it was a disaster. For most of the sixteen months I served in Korea, we also did not receive any fresh eggs. In the chow line each morning, if you wanted eggs, you got scrambled dehydrated eggs. They came in liquid form in a can and there was no preparation possible other than scrambling. When served, they were invariably green in color. When I had children and read to them, I always assumed that Dr. Seuss (who had served in World War II) had drawn his inspiration for not liking *Green Eggs* and *Ham* from his military service – like our uniforms and equipment, dehydrated eggs had also been standard issue in World War II. As they did not tempt the palate from 1940-1945, so they did not in Korea. Indeed, when we finally got fresh eggs in Korea, soldiers who had never liked eggs before now found them palatable and even pleasing. Anyway, between liver and green eggs, a lot of guys ate a lot of toast or bread with coffee that week. Somewhere around the same time, we also, literally, ran out of toilet paper. Initially,

Time magazine, Far East edition, proved to be an adequate substitute for those of us who subscribed. It was printed on very thin paper. But, after a day or two, that was no longer available. We then turned to the most readily available source of paper. From the jaws of every mill, of every intercept operator, spewed forth multiple copies of every word intercepted. Between every two sheets of paper there emerged, only to be discarded, reams of carbon paper. The use of carbon paper was no more than marginally tricky when employed in an outhouse in daylight. At two o'clock in the morning, in an unlit outhouse with matches or flashlight, the ability to be sure that one had correctly identified the shiny side of the carbon paper was a rather more parlous question. The results, on occasion, were a cause for black despair.

Between the humdrum, the comical, the annoying and the infuriating, the days, weeks and months rolled by. Some things were recurrent. The Army's constant fear of venereal disease produced, at least in the 326th, one odd, even ironic, result. In what was, I believe, an effort to prevent venereal disease, the Army (or some of its officers) broke its own regulations. About every six to eight weeks, a "dance" was held. Two or three truckloads of "working girls" were brought into the encampment for several hours and then sent back home. We all assumed that the women had been medically examined before they were imported. When the trucks rolled out, there was a virtual cascade, like salmon back to spawn, of off-duty soldiers jumping fences and waving the trucks down to jump on board and pursue the *inamorata* of the evening. Troops pulling guard duty at the time had to work hard to avoid cricks in their necks from turning away.

More time passed and soon we were "short timers," with only a month or two left to serve in Korea. Already, most of our friends had completed their tours and headed home. Then, the orders came and, once again, we cleared post, with many fewer hoops to jump through or boxes to check. Then we began our trip home. Those leaving from the 326th, went into Seoul and joined other members of the 501st Group who were leaving and then on to the port of embarkation. For one last time, the Army's fixation with venereal disease impinged on our lives. We were subjected to one last, mass "short arm" inspection. I assume that the short arm inspection has vanished along with the *Brown Shoe Army*. I can think of no way in which it could persist in a gender neutral Army. In any event, a large number of us, scores, if not hundreds, were gathered in a large dockside warehouse. We were required to unbutton the flies of our trousers (no fatigue uniforms had zippers then) and display our penises. We then walked past a soldier (who I assume had some medical training) and submitted to a visual inspection. Uncircumcised troops were required to maneuver the foreskin to display the glans. Once that quite demeaning process was completed, we were cleared to embark and head home.

In that older, *Brown Shoe Army*, we sailed for home; we did not fly. Unlike the individual trooper heading home from Viet Nam, who could find himself going from combat to Mom's kitchen in seventy-two or ninety-six hours, we were at sea for between one and two weeks. In my shipment there were, obviously, relatively few men who had seen combat but many of us had seen its immediate aftermath and results. The long journey, surrounded by men who had all shared comparative experiences provided a means of decompression and a transition back to a civilian world. I have often thought that a similar experience of shared memories might have made the trip back to "the world" less traumatic for those Viet Nam vets than it proved to be. Unbeknown to us, even as we embarked, was that our Army was already dying. Orders and contracts had already been placed for the green uniforms of the "new Army" – though in order to use up stocks on hand, the new uniforms would not be issued until 1957.

The voyage home was not without incident. A few days out from Korea, we ran into a typhoon that stayed with us for nearly two full days. It was an experience we would happily have done without. When the storm struck, the troops were sent below to their berthing compartments and required to remain there. In addition to heavy seas and strong winds, the ship also pitched and tossed erratically, at the mercy of the seas. Then, about two o'clock in the morning, there came a terrifying series of noises of incredible volume ringing throughout the ship. It was almost as if someone or something was trying to break through the ship's hull. As we were later to discover, a cargo boom had broken loose and was battering itself against the superstructure. Of course, in those dark hours we did not know that, nor did anyone tell us, leaving us to construct many possible variants on what was happening and why.

Rationally, it is obvious, that the best thing to do with the troops was to keep them below and out of the crew's way. It is also obvious that dealing with riotous seas and the errant cargo boom was the proper use of the crew's energy and skills. As we awaited our fate below, however, few of us were immediately wedded to logic or to the admiration of the intensity of the crew's focus on the problems at hand. In any event, the storm drew away, the seas calmed and we arrived in Seattle, Washington, where we proceeded to debark. We were back in the United States and damned happy to be there. We had returned to Seattle, rather than San Francisco. For the romantics among us, the fact that we did not sail in "under that Golden Gate" was a disappointment of sorts, but didn't hold a candle to being back. Underneath a sort of Humphrey Bogart cynicism, I believe we were all deeply moved. I know that ever since that November day I have always had a soft spot in my heart for Seattle – though I have only returned a couple of times.

After disembarkation, we were loaded into buses, because, once again, we had to be processed. To give the Army its due, this was the fastest and most efficient disposal and dispersal of troops I ever saw. I do not remember whether we went to Fort Lewis or Fort Lawton; both were then active posts in the Seattle area. It was a thoughtful process. Somewhere in all the activity since leaving the 326th, we had once again been issued Class A uniforms, including our low quarters (dress shoes) so we were again physically a *Brown Shoe Army*. The Army had also taken it into account that Thanksgiving was on the horizon. We were all to receive a thirty-day, disembarkation, leave. However, since that would involve reporting to a new duty station just before Christmas, with consequent administrative awkwardness, our leaves were extended several days, to bring us on to our new posts after January 1st, when most offices would be fully operational. We all received pay for our month on leave, and virtually all of us also received the one or two months' back pay due to us.

We also were entitled to travel pay. In that regard, you indicated that you planned to travel from Seattle to your home of record by plane, train or automobile. The choice determined both the amount of money you would receive and the number of days allotted for travel home. Thus, if you chose to say you would fly, you got one or two days and the price of a ticket. The few old timers among us had already told us to choose automobile. In that case you received a stipulated amount of money (by way of illustration, let us say thirteen cents a mile for something in the range of 2,500 miles from Seattle to the East Coast), plus many more days were allotted, and not charged against leave time. More days, and more money! We took their advice. All of this, though efficiently done, required time. Time standing in line, signing for monies received and various other administrative procedures dear to the hearts of bureaucrats everywhere. Since an entire ship load of troops could not be at the same place at the same time, barracks were opened for us to use to wait between various processes, to use the latrines and to rest. Once the money, all, of course, in cash, began to flow, the private rooms usually assigned to platoon sergeants, almost immediately became mini-casinos primarily showcasing high stakes poker games.

At this distance in time, I would suggest that each trooper was in possession of at least $300.00, and some perhaps $600.00 or more. I was a staff sergeant at that time and my pay was roughly $150.00 a month. Once you figure leave pay, back pay and travel pay, it was, in 1954, more money than most of us had ever seen before. To understand that number, gasoline was twenty-two cents a gallon, a loaf of bread cost about fifteen cents and a quart of milk was twenty-one cents. Perhaps then more directly relevant, beer was five or ten cents a glass.

I had thought of sitting in on a game; I had not fared too badly in barracks poker games over the previous two years where one might win or lose twenty or thirty dollars in a couple of hours. As I sought a seat,

I realized that drawing cards required a twenty dollar ante, and Helen Kelly's son decided that he was not destined for the world of high stakes poker. The results were predictable. Hours later, as we were leaving post, I ran into a fellow who was trying to figure out how long it would take him to hitchhike to Alabama, and whether he would be able to eat at least one meal a day.

A small group of us, primarily ASA and bound for New York City and New Jersey, managed to get hold of a taxi (they were at a premium) and set off for the Seattle airport. We had, of course, all said we were driving, but all fully intended to fly. The process, while standard, was ethically dubious and brought us not only extra money, which was of minor importance, but extra time at home after almost a year and a half away. As it turned out, the next flight bound for the NY Metropolitan area was on *Northwest Airlines*, and not due out for four or five hours. It was also fully booked. *Northwest* personnel seemed genuinely solicitous of returning soldiers. They suggested that we fly standby and promised to do their best for us. That left us with several hours to kill and very little to do. Young as we were, I had just turned nineteen in August, we realized that drinking and traveling standby were contraindicated. We managed to kill about a full hour in the airport barbershop. Each of us signed up for a shave, a haircut, a facial and a manicure. I think the total cost, with a good tip, was less than ten dollars each. After that, we decided that we had killed enough time that perhaps we could have one beer, and so we headed to the nearest airport bar. Air travel has changed a great deal since those days but one thing that seems stable is that in an airport a bar is never very distant. As we grabbed a table, an elderly man (perhaps sixty or so – my standards of what constitutes elderly have significantly altered since then) came over and asked us if we were just back from Korea. I assume our O.D. uniforms and happy faces were indicators for frequent fliers. We said, "Yes sir." He asked if he might join us and buy us a drink. Not averse to the idea of a free drink, we welcomed him with enthusiasm. He represented both an "attaboy" and largesse.

At some point, he began to praise Syngman Rhee, then the President of South Korea, as a great democratic leader. Our time in Korea had exposed us to the various political machinations of Rhee and his Liberal Party organization. Among many allegations, which seemed confirmed by events, were highly dubious, if not dictatorial changes in the national constitution, as well as the literal disappearance of an opponent during an election campaign. (Happily, the candidate did reappear, but only after Rhee's party had triumphed.) We brought these facts to our new friend's attention. In fact, it is possible that I, specifically, did so. In what would turn out to be my first experience with what came to be called "McCarthyism," I was immediately dismissed as a fellow traveler, a "pinko," if not indeed a Communist. Quite naively, I pointed out that I possessed a top secret security clearance. That statement was greeted merely as evidence of how deeply our national security apparatus had been penetrated. We were offered no further drinks, which one or two of my colleagues clearly held against me. The drink, the barbershop and the resilience of youth, however, enabled us to rather quickly forget the tension the moment had created and quite soon, thereafter, our flight was called.

All of us, standby or not, were seated and began the journey east. As was the norm in those days, the flight made two or three stops as we crossed the continent, but our luck held and we all made it home. Wishing one another well, we parted and went our separate ways. Having called from Seattle, I spent my first night back in New York on Perry Avenue in the Bronx, at my Aunt Anne's apartment. It was a lovely occasion, and I was feted and made much of. However, as my mother might have said, to make sure that my ego did not crush my humility, as I basked in the glow of family and fellowship, the family cat wandered over and clawed my hand. The following day, I took the subway to Grand Central Terminal, grabbed a train to New Rochelle and headed to my father's flat.

As I returned to New Rochelle, I was unaware what a significant role it was to play in my life. In the course of the next eight years, I would matriculate and graduate from college in that city. There I would meet and fall in love with the woman with whom I would spend the rest of my life. There, we would welcome the first three of our children. It was also as a resident of New Rochelle that I would begin my career as a teacher. All that lay ahead, but as I got off the New York, New Haven and Hartford Railroad that day, I was primarily concerned, even anxious, about the relationship my father and I were to have. Ours had always been an uneasy one, made possible really by my mother as both a person and as a social emollient. After her death, we had coexisted in large part because I was not yet able to be truly independent, but also because I was no longer small enough to be physically quieted. It had certainly worked best when he moved to Westchester and I stayed in Buffalo. In fairness, it should be pointed out that it was he who made that arrangement possible. It was he who found and paid for my room and board during my senior year in high school. It worked very well for both of us – though I shudder to think what a modern child protective services bureaucrat would make of it. As it was to turn out, after I was discharged, we lived together but saw little of one another. I was to be at Iona most of the day and working at least one part-time job at night. I suppose the relationship might be described as "guarded but correct." We shared space but rarely, when awake, at the exact same time. We were, virtually always, civil but rarely, if ever, warm.

If our relationship in this period was relatively even and benign, it may have been due to the fact that we saw relatively little of one another as I have indicated – but it may also have been due to the fact that my father was engaged in a courtship. My mother had now been dead for four years and my father had met a woman, an immigrant from Great Britain, in whom he was very interested. I no longer remember the lady's name, but she had migrated with her daughter, and her mother. The daughter called Mary, was quite a pretty girl, perhaps a year or so younger than I. My father, at that time was forty-eight, so I assume that Mary's mother was of a similar age and the grandmother probably in her early seventies.

Shortly after my arrival in New Rochelle, I was introduced to all of them. All were pleasant, even charming. It soon became evident that the courting couple believed that efforts should be made to involve Tom and Mary in a dating relationship. I think it is fair to say that, while neither of us was revolted by the idea, neither were we enthusiastic about it. I think we may have gone out twice. The more memorable of the two was in Manhattan at the nightclub where Guy Lombardo and his band were the house band. The young lady was both decorative and decorous. We both found that we had little in common – other than our parents' wishes that we like one another. I do remember that she was very fond of a song, then very popular, called *Cherry Pink and Apple Blossom White.* Maybe the second date was a movie. By that time we were comfortable with one another and had reached the mutual conclusion that there was not and would not be any spark between us, and we did not need to further test that hypothesis.

Her grandmother did become the center of a very good story. The trio was on the cusp of being naturalized as citizens at this time. The great day arrived for them to appear, take the oath and be sworn in as citizens. Up until President Obama's decree in 2015, all prospective citizens had been asked if they were prepared to support the U.S. in conflict against their former country. When Mary's grandmother was asked if she would bear arms against Britain, she supposedly replied, "Don't be silly, Your Honor – but if a little bit of typing would help."

My father and I did have one early confrontation. When I arrived, knowing no one other than my father, there was little to attract me or to hold me in New Rochelle. It took me a day or two to take care of a few practical matters. For example, in a used furniture store. I located a handsome chest on chest in which to keep most of my clothing. After the passage of sixty years, I still have it. Once I had it in the flat, I asked my father where I would find the shirts, slacks, etc., I had left behind when I enlisted. It turned out that they were no longer available. Somehow in the twenty-seven months I had been gone, they had vanished. As best as I could gather, my father had generously donated some of it to those he felt in need, and otherwise disposed of the rest. After a short period of intense anger, I persuaded myself that since I was probably an inch taller than when I was seventeen and somewhat more filled out as well, that much of it would no longer have been a good fit. Still, there had been a few items which I had really liked. Shortly thereafter, I went to a men's clothing store (*Bonds*), quite near Grand Central Terminal. For less than $300.00, I got a suit, a sports jacket, several pairs of slacks, a couple of shirts and ties and a Raglan style tweed topcoat. For some reason, I also bought a pair of pigskin gloves, which I liked but never found much use for. Allowing a few days for alterations, I thought myself a well-dressed man indeed!

I then thought of another chore which needed to be taken care of (and which might also allow for a practical joke). I hied myself off to the New Rochelle draft board. The law required that all males had to register for the draft by the age of (I think) eighteen and one-half. That time had come upon me while I was in Korea and this was, indeed, my first opportunity to fulfill the letter of the law. Most local draft boards in those days were staffed by one or two middle-aged to elderly ladies who, with an odd pencil or two and a typewriter, managed to sustain the nation's military establishment. Seeking an effect, I donned my new clothes (not omitting the pigskin gloves) and presented myself at the Selective Service office. I was pleasantly greeted by the woman who seemed to be the complete staff, I told her I had come to register. After I had provided my name and address, she asked my date of birth. August 13, 1935, I replied. The date clearly indicated that I was at least nine months late in appearing. Clearly uncomfortable, she explained the letter of the law and asked why I was late. I replied, I thought quite non-chalantly, that I had been busy. Her anxiety, on my behalf, at this point was so obvious that I could not continue the game. I quickly explained that I had been in Korea, where there was no USSS office, and provided her with my military ID. She was very gracious, and I quickly passed from the "smart aleck" who had entered the office into a chagrined and chastened young man. I really have never been good at practical jokes.

I had never lost sight of the idea that after my enlistment was over, I would leave the Army, go to college and graduate school and prepare myself for a career as a college professor of history. With about nine months to go until discharge, it logically seemed time to begin those preparations. Going to college sixty years ago was not the anxiety-producing, all-consuming, exercise it has since become. Knowing, for example, that I would be enlisting after high school, I never felt it necessary to take any SAT or other examinations – at this distance, I'm not even sure that I knew such exams existed.

So, in a state of innocence, I headed up North Avenue in New Rochelle to Iona College. I need to remind myself again, what a different world it was in 1955. It had, for example, literally never occurred to me to explore the academic market place, although I was within an hour's distance of colleges ranging from the Ivy League, Columbia, through CCNY and NYU, as well as smaller institutions such as Fordham and Manhattan. I was in New Rochelle and Iona College was in New Rochelle. Ergo…. (The College of New Rochelle was also there, but it was a "girl's" school.) Iona it would be. It was an all-male college ("boy's" school) of Roman Catholic auspices, run by the Irish Christian Brothers. Timon had been the same and, of course the *Brown Shoe Army,* aside from an occasional WAC viewed in the far distance had also been. I obtained and filled out the necessary papers and returned them to the admission's office. I also made clear to admissions that I had never taken SATs and that, if an entrance examination was required, I would need lead time, as I would have to obtain a three-day pass to sit the exam. As I now think of it, I am struck by the fact that the notion of being denied admission never crossed my mind. Certainly, I sought no alternative. Such, I suppose, is the arrogance of youth. I might add that some of my contemporaries, colleagues and family might append an additional clause to the preceding sentence.

Having regularized my status with the draft board and started the college admissions process, I found myself on vacation. I had a roof over my head, in my father's flat, the start of a "few sticks of furniture" and, at least for the next nine months, regular employment. After that, there would be the GI Bill. The GI Bill constituted regular monthly payments from the U.S. Government for veterans who were enrolled in and in good standing in an accredited educational institution. At that time, I think it paid around $210.00 per month. Iona's tuition was $250.00 per semester. As a single student, I would draw about $2,000.00 or so a year, with tuition payments of $500.00 and the remainder for books and other necessities and for living expenses. (All of these being round number approximations.) At the moment, I had a bit more than a month of compensated loafing ahead of me. In a way, it was a reprise of the summer of 1952. I spent a good deal of time with various Kanes and Kellys. I always felt welcome in each of the households and was now, by and large, treated as an adult, even a privileged adult. I had been out of the nest for more than two years, had military service, and had traveled farther around the world than anyone in either family in my own generation or that of my parents. My Aunt Kitty's husband, Charlie Murphy was a close second. He was in the shipping business and had, prior to World War II done some business in the Philippines. This new, somewhat elevated status was a pleasant reality, made more so by the fact that it entailed neither duty nor responsibility. Once again, I bounced between the Bronx, Rutherford and Norwalk. Once again, I joined my Uncle Joe and Marjorie's husband Bill at the *American Legion* bar in Norwalk – though now, I too had tales of military service and service humor to tell. In any event, Thanksgiving and then Christmas came, were appropriately celebrated and went. As always, they were occasions of warmth and good humor.

New Year's Eve, 1954-55, on the other hand, was destined to be a most unusual occasion. A friend of mine from Korea, let's call him Leon, was also celebrating his return "stateside," and he had decided to host a New Year's Eve party. It was to be held in a hotel just off Times Square, and I was invited. It seemed a perfect fit. Just as George M. Cohan had said, it was "only forty-five minutes away" from New Rochelle and then a brisk walk from Grand Central to Times Square, avoid all but the fringe of the holiday crowd, a nod to the famous statue of Father Duffy of the old "Fighting 69th" and on into the hotel. There I met a group of other young people (of course, I didn't know them, but then I didn't know anyone else either) a couple of drinks and welcome in 1955. What could be wrong with that?

Leon had brought a date, a girl called Rhonda, to the party. She seemed very pleasant, as did the other guests. I got a beer and began to circulate. It quickly became clear that I was perhaps the only guest who was not from Brooklyn. As a *Dodgers* fan of some standing, that seemed no problem. Once again, alcohol would prove to have the ability to cause a pleasant, even placid, party to explode. One of the female guests drank too much and became first an annoyance and then, rather quickly, a major pain. Leon, who, like the rest of us was also drinking, struggled manfully to placate the girl but she proved to be strongly resistant to reason. Becoming angry, in a dramatic gesture, he reached into a closet, grabbed what he thought was her coat and told her to "put on her damn coat and get out." Like many dramatic gestures, this one too proved to be ill-advised. As it turned out, he had mistakenly grabbed Rhonda's coat and, for whatever reason, she took it seriously, responded to him angrily and burst into tears. He was unable to convince her that it was a mistake, made in all innocence. (I suppose, risking redundancy, it should be noted, that she too had been drinking.)

After much bickering, Leon asked me to intercede for him and try to calm Rhonda down. She stood by the door, clutching her coat and whimpering. I guess, as the only stranger at the party, I seemed a logical possibility as mediator. There seemed to be little option, so I agreed. I located a bit of semiprivate space, persuaded Rhonda to join me and we began to talk. With Leon out of sight, the weeping diminished and died away. I told her, several times and in different terms, that Leon , justifiably angry with the other girl, had just gotten hold of the wrong coat and that he was deeply sorry and that he was aware that her feelings had been hurt, which he had never intended. She vociferously maintained that he had wronged her and that she wanted to go home. I told her that Leon had sung her praises to me, how attractive she was, and how warm and gracious. I repeatedly spoke of his regret. While her opinion never changed, she did become calmer and the conversation less emotional. After twenty or thirty minutes, I became aware that the conversation had shifted and that I had become the subject. I was, unlike Leon, sweet and considerate. I was also easy to talk to and cute. In fact, she said, the best solution to the current situation would be if we both left the party and I took her home to Brooklyn. She would be very happy and grateful if I did that. I now tried, rather frantically, to get back to Leon's affection for her, his genuine contrition for the mix-up and anything else I could think of to refocus her attention. At last, in sheer desperation, I informed her that I was not about to head for Brooklyn at that hour of the morning of New Year's Day. Indeed, I quite ungallantly pointed out, I would have to leave soon to catch my train back to New Rochelle. It was a bit of a stretch, but I cherished it as my way out. Soon after, I reported utter failure to Leon and headed for Grand Central Terminal and a train. By then, I don't think Leon was thinking much about Rhonda anyway. And so I welcomed 1955, not the best New Year's Eve ever but certainly an unforgettable one.

In a few days, it was time for another train, this one for Boston, where I changed trains and headed toward Worcester and Fort Devens. If anything, the next eight months were even more boring than the six months in 1953 had been. The fact was that the Korean War was over, the military was being drastically cut back, and no one was sure what to do with us. When I reported in at Headquarters upon my arrival, I was subject to a sad sight. There, sitting at a desk, typing industriously away, was an elderly Corporal whom I recognized as my basic training company commander, then Captain Gallagher. The best bet was that he had been caught in a RIF (Reduction In Force) where reserve officers (those lacking commissions in the Regular Army) with long service were offered a sort of "Hobson's Choice," leave the Army now, or accept a reduction in rank to your last permanent enlisted rank (usually as a non-com) and complete the number of years remaining until retirement, whereupon you would retire with your pension based upon the highest rank you had held. RIFs were almost customary when the Army needed to reduce its size. I found Gallagher's status quite embarrassing and, though I am sure he would never have recognized me, I studiously avoided going anywhere near him. "Galloping Gallagher" a clerk-typist!

As we reported in, drew bunks and bedding and otherwise established our existence, we became numerically something like one-half or two-thirds of a platoon. We were assigned to the same barracks and, at least nominally, placed under the command of a Warrant Officer. In fact, we virtually never saw or interacted with him. Our duties, such as they were, involved writing communications traffic to be sent as part of communications problems, sand table exercises or maneuvers. It was the kind of "chatter" that Army units usually generate, and we could have done it in our sleep – perhaps we did. For example, the Red Cross asks that Private Jones be granted compassionate leave to be with his dying mother, the QM (Quartermaster) requisitions a gross of spark plugs, Private Beauregard is designated Regimental Soldier of the Month, interspersed with movement orders, personnel matters and the like. All these messages were to be used in exercises of one sort or another to lend verisimilitude, as similar ones had been used in 1944 to validate FUSAG. It was what we would do for the next seven to eight months. It was totally without challenge or interest and it was boring beyond belief.

There was one saving grace: most of us occupied the ranks of E-5 or higher; which was that we were non-commissioned officers (in the Army of 1955, an E-5 was a staff sergeant) and as such, we always "had a pass in our pocket." That meant that outside duty hours we were free to leave the post at any time and, unless specifically assigned a duty, our weekends were free. One odd result of the percentage of us with sergeant stripes, was that the few PFCs and Corporals among us ended up functioning as "gofers." It was they who went out for coffee or ran other errands.

Given its downsizing, the Army was surprisingly diligent in trying to persuade us to re-enlist. Indeed, they even tried a species of bribery or blackmail to persuade us to "re-up." The emerging black shoe Army had already begun a series of changes, and one of those was the establishment of Specialist ranks. When we had enlisted, anyone promoted to E-4 had become a Corporal, the lowest of the non-commissioned officer ranks. Under the new system, an E-4 might become a Corporal, or he might become a Specialist.

When we were approached to re-enlist, we were told, if you re-enlist, you may keep your rank as a non-com; if not, you must accept the equivalent specialist rank and insignia. Even those of us who had adapted well to the Army failed to find the offer either fair or attractive and so, we became specialists – same pay, less prestige. The regret was, of course, primarily psychological: we were all scheduled for discharge before the end of the year. It was real enough, though, that some years later I would briefly serve in an active reserve unit, at least partially in order to reclaim my old rank of Staff Sergeant.

As I have implied, our duty function seemed to us to be nominal, as was the degree of supervision we received. A normal day would see us report to our work place – essentially no more than a large open barrack space (essentially an empty squad bay), with tables and mills, between 09:00 and 09:30 each day. The Warrant Officer to whom we nominally reported had his office on the floor above, though we rarely saw him. After arrival, we would send someone out for coffee, Danish, doughnuts and newspapers. Those of us who had not yet done so would shave. By 10:30 or thereabouts, having eaten and chatted, at least some of us would be at work. We wrote "traffic" until 12:00 or 12:30 and then went to lunch. Returning around 14:00, we would prepare some more administrative messages. To the best of my memory, we were never asked to improve either the quality or quantity of our product. What we did and how we did it was a matter of our own judgment. Often, even the few hours that we "worked" became too onerous, and we indulged ourselves. On one occasion, we spent several days amusing ourselves by typing up a list of all the comic strips and/or characters we had ever read or heard of. At first, the examples came faster than we could type, but after a couple of hours, recollection slowed. We kept one mill and its long paper roll for the cartoons and, when we were stymied, we would create traffic for the Army. Then someone would come up with another character or strip, and we would be off again as that stimulated someone else's memory. I no longer remember the number we reached but I am sure it was well above two hundred, from *Tilly the Toiler* to *Terry and the Pirates.* At some point our interest waned or our memories failed, and we moved on.

Usually between 15:30 and 16:00 hours, we would terminate our "working" day and close up shop. Sometimes we would leave post and go for a drive, other times back to the barracks for a nap or just a bull-session until chow time. Chow was pretty much the same from Camp Kilmer to Korea and back, but this tour at Devens did offer one burst of the bizarre. For some reason, perhaps economy, one night a week, the mess hall offered up C-Rations. These canned meals had been prepared for troops in the field, from World War II through Korea. Some of those we were eating in 1955, we were told by the KPs, dated to World War II. One C-Ration night, I had wandered into the chow hall, looked at the various pans of Ham and Lima Beans, Pork Patties, etc., and decided I would skip chow. My mother would have said my Guardian Angel was watching over me that night. For hours, ambulances pulled in and out of the Company area as sick troopers were carried off to have their stomachs pumped. Most evenings, on the other hand, involved quiet nights, reading in the barracks or maybe watching TV in the Company recreation room or nights in various inns and road houses in search of both alcohol and female companionship. On other occasions, we would drive up to New Hampshire and tour scenic spots in the White Mountains. In many ways it now seems like a rehearsal for retirement (in my case, at nineteen). It was somewhere between boring and idyllic. The year rolled on; winter gave way to spring and spring to summer. I celebrated my twentieth birthday, quite quietly, and suddenly I realized my enlistment was ending.

In the meantime, my various communications with the Iona College Admissions Office in regard to admissions testing brought a letter that said, "relax." There will be no need for an admissions test. We have chatted with the faculty and administration at Timon High School and we look forward to meeting you at matriculation of the Class of 1959. Report on campus on Sept. …, 1955.

For the last time, I began to clear post. I had medical clearances, some sort of advice/guidance about life after the Army and I signed for clothing and equipment I would take with me. (We all still had at least a technical commitment to five years in the inactive reserve.)

Other equipment (e.g., bedding) was returned to the Supply Sergeant and, on August 20, 1955, I left Fort Devens and the Army.

It was not an auspicious day. Hurricane Diane had ravaged New England the day before, leaving considerable devastation in its wake. Westfield, MA, for example, got 19+ inches of rain. I was hitchhiking, complete with full duffel bag (all those uniforms and boots – all still *brown shoe* of course). The wake of the storm necessitated a highly circuitous route. I ended up having to head east until I got to the coast and US Route 1, the old Boston Post Road, which seemed to be the only route still open to get me out of New England and into New York. (It should be kept in mind that the modern national road system did not then exist; though President Eisenhower was about to propose it.) In passing, I might note that hitchhiking, now seemingly largely gone, was then regularly practiced, and that it was rare for a soldier in uniform to go more than about ten minutes without being picked up. Still, on that day it was the best part of twelve hours before I reached New Rochelle where I would begin another phase of the story.

CHAPTER 6
Home: New Rochele, Iona, Dorothy – Undergraduate

When I awoke in my father's flat in New Rochelle on August 21st, 1955, I was at least intellectually aware that I was about to begin an important new phase in my life. I was totally unaware that it would also mark the beginning of another, equally significant, change: love and marriage. I had about two weeks until Labor Day, which would usher in my freshman year in college. There would be no time now for a leisurely round of visiting with Kanes or Kellys, just a few quick hellos and "welcome homes." There was time, however, for a brief, if somewhat intense, conversation with my father. As I have indicated, I had always intended to study and teach history. That was the major I had chosen at Iona. My father, on the other hand, was avid in his desire that I should become an accountant. Iona, by the way, had an excellent reputation in accounting. Our discussion was based on his belief that I was throwing my life away by majoring in history. It was not practical. In the last twenty or so years of his life, he was a clerk/ bookkeeper and clearly he wanted me to do better, to step up to the level of those who were his bosses. One of the debts I owe to the Army was that those three years provided me with the GI Bill of Rights. I was my own man and the choices I made would be mine. I was never angry over this discussion – I knew my father was concerned, at least primarily, that I have a more prosperous life than his. Still, at the end, I knew he thought me something of a fool.

I set about my preparation for college by scouting out a serviceable used typewriter at an acceptable price. It was a '30s or '40s vintage model: a square, giant machine which was in excellent condition. It would serve me for well over a decade. Immediately, however, it did present a problem. I had no car, nor did I know anyone in New Rochelle from whom I could beg a ride. While I had money on hand, I had no way of knowing when I might receive the first payments from the Veteran's Administration for my college expenses. It seemed ill-advised then to take a cab with the type-writer. The distance from the shop to our Franklin St. flat was probably about a mile and a half. I decided that the wisest course was to carry it home. It was handed to me in a cardboard box, and off I went. As I walked, the machine grew heavier. By the time I was half way, it seemed to weigh fifty pounds or more. By the time I started up the stairs (it was a third floor walkup) it weighed at least one hundred pounds. By the time I was finally able to set it down on a table, I really loathed that typewriter.

As opposed to that effort, everything else I needed to learn or do was astonishingly easy. The walk to the bus stop where I would catch the bus up North Ave. to Iona was only a two or three block walk as were the laun-dry and the barbershop which my father and I used. Assembling the few items I needed was really rather simple, aided by the fact that the khaki trousers of my summer uniforms served splendidly as pairs of slacks, at least until the weather turned colder. Similarly, my Army field jacket, with and without its liner, gave excellent service through the fall and winter. The field jacket also proved useful to me in another way. As is evident, I per-formed virtually all necessary tasks on foot. On one occasion, as I was heading down Main St. toward Franklin Ave., I passed a woman walking a full sized French Poodle. A few steps after I passed her, I felt a sort of punch in my back, as the dog leaped to attack me. Because I was wearing my field jacket, he got mostly fabric and none of me.

Like the chow and my boyhood sledding experience, the incident did not turn me into an *aficionado* of Albert Payson Terhune's various books about wonderful dogs.

I don't recall any great emotional feeling about starting my college education; it was rather a "this is the next necessary step" feeling. Shortly after Labor Day I presented myself at Iona and stood in the requisite lines and after the necessary preliminaries was handed a 3 x 5 card upon which my class schedule for the fall term had been typed. A class schedule, even for freshmen, is, today, something of a negotiated document, subject to change; even tweaked several times between registration and the start of classes. In 1955, it was more a *diktat*, from the administration to the student. In any event, at day's end I had matriculated.

Iona College, as it was in 1955, is now a memory. It was then an all-male commuter's college with about 1700 undergraduates. It had no dormitories at all. It was a Roman Catholic college, operated under the auspices of the Irish Christian Brothers. As a History major, my recollection is that I was required to complete a minimum of 19 credits in Philosophy, either 18 or 21 in English, 2 credits in Religion each semester, 6 credits in Math and 6 in Science, 12 in Modern Languages, 12 in Social Sciences and, I believe, 3 in Fine Arts. The major required either 30 or 36. In any case, a "normal" academic load per semester was six courses, usually five for 3 credits each and a 2 credit load for the Religion course.

I began the semester with enthusiasm and, for the most part found myself interested and involved throughout the term. At the end, I presented a record of 4 As and 2 Cs, for a Grade Point Average (GPA) of about 3.3.

In addition to academic work, I found myself, once again, trying to create some sort of social network, initially at or through Iona. The Korean War had now been over for two years and those of us who entered the college as veterans in 1955 had been discharged after either three or four year enlistments. As such, we found ourselves the last, or nearly the last, large bunch of Korean War veterans. Our shared military experiences set us apart and provided an obvious bond and so we tended to group. Iona also played a role in the grouping process, in that those of us who were Liberal Arts majors, or Business Majors, or Science Majors, tended to be in many of the same classes. Since, however, the Iona of that era was truly a small college, there tended to be a sort of spillover effect, particularly among required core courses. Among the veterans, there was also a major exception to the clique aspect. There was a member of our class, who was just sixteen, called Paul Fritz, who became for us a sort of younger brother/mascot. While he was almost always among us, he was a very bright young man who certainly had no need for academic assistance from us. Rather, we enjoyed his company and his zest for life. We may have added a dollop of experience and maturity to his growth: no more than that.

As for me, gradually some faces and some personalities came to be familiar, comfortable and trusted factors in my life. Ray Kelly, for example, would later be one of my groomsmen. In Iona's then current identification system, I was 55A4. I had matriculated in 1955, I was an Arts major and, I assume I was the fourth Kelly in the Arts Division. Ray was probably the second or third. For obvious reasons, then, including the facts that we were both veterans and history majors in September of 1955, we found ourselves in a number of the same classes.

Off campus, there were other eventualities to be dealt with. While the money from the G I GI Bill would more than adequately cover tuition, books and some living expenses, other costs loomed large – as did the need for some sort of supplemental income. I needed to find a job. Fortunately, not too far down Main St. from Franklin Ave. (probably about ½ to ¾ of a mile, quite walkable) there was a busy *Howard Johnson's Restaurant*. Now nearly gone, the restaurants and "motor lodges" were in the 1950s nearly ubiquitous. The then famous orange roofs rather guaranteed acceptable lodging and reasonably priced and decent food. The chain boasted the taste of its hot dogs and the fact that it offered no fewer than twenty-six flavors of ice cream. As it happened, their needs and mine happily coincided. They were in need of what they called a "counterman." A counterman served customers at the counter; which was a long, relatively low surface with perhaps a dozen or so stools directly in front. There, individual customers would sit while they ordered and consumed what they wished. Some, only a cup of coffee, others a milk shake and, still others, a full meal. At some level, I was always amused and fully aware, that a counterman was a euphemism for a "soda jerk."

The facility also included a full service restaurant, staffed by uniformed waitresses. Countermen wore white shirts, dark slacks and ties and a sort of paper overseas cap. The waitresses, most of whom were in their later teens and twenties, supplemented their salaries with tips. Indeed, the salaries were so low that it might be more correct to say the salaries supplemented the tips. Countermen were paid more but received little or nothing in the way of tips. I should also mention that, while working a shift, one got a free meal. I usually worked late afternoons and/or evenings. We were, I think, open till 9:00 p.m. It was my first, adult, civilian job and, for the most part, I enjoyed it.

There were, of course, annoyances. It was a rare day when we did not see at least one self-satisfied customer who wanted us to recite the entire list of the twenty-six flavors – despite the fact that that they were displayed, in large letters on the wall behind the counter. It was usually just easier to recite the list to him (they were virtually always male) than to argue. One could be reasonably sure that those individuals would not leave a tip. After closing, we cleaned up before we left. For me, that portion of the evening was usually fairly pleasant. As we worked, the waitresses would almost always play their favorite tunes on the juke box. On occasion, they might even dance a little bit as they worked. The countermen, there were usually two on duty, might even find themselves being flirted with a bit – not too seriously; in the pecking order, countermen did not rank with waitresses, but there was socialization – and that was pleasant enough.

It also represented a significant change for me. After moving from pillar to post between 1948 and 1952, followed by three years in the Army, I now found myself establishing another new group of friends. This one, however, allowing for the fact that Iona was another all male institution, would include female members of the species. I found that a marked improvement and I was determined to embrace it. I did, briefly, date one of the waitresses, called Kitty. She was fresh from Ireland and, yes, she did have red hair. She was what my mother would have called "a slip of a girl." No more than 5' 1" tall, I doubt that she weighed much over 100 pounds. We went out a few times, mostly to movies - I still had no car, or access to one. It was no more than fun, some companionship, some conversation and perhaps a bit of what my mother (again) would have called "slap and tickle."

In those days, women's colleges still held what were called "tea dances." Held in the late afternoon, they were designed to offer the "young ladies" (that's the term they used) an opportunity to meet and mingle, under controlled circumstances, with young men of approved background (by this time largely defined simply as also being college undergraduates). New Rochelle's local Catholic woman's college (The College of New Rochelle - CNR) posted notices of tea dances at Iona. I decided to attend. Suitably attired, I presented myself and registered. I was then presented to the young woman whose escort I was to be. She was attractive, sweet and astonishingly boring. Or, perhaps I bored her. In any event, we danced a few dances (a skill which I have never fully mastered), the afternoon came to an end and I never found it necessary to return to CNR socially.

I also explored other avenues which would enable me to broaden my social horizons. One of those involved the New Rochelle *American Legion* post. Shortly after I got to New Rochelle, my father began to suggest that I should seek membership in the local *Legion* post. As time passed, his suggestions became stronger and stronger. I realized that he was hoping to gain access to the post and its bar through me. I have always assumed that he hoped to find the kind of companionship there that his brother Joe and Bill Surrette had at the *Legion* post in Norwalk. Finally, I agreed and I joined the *American Legion*. It didn't work out well for Dad. He could only get in if I accompanied him, and I was working five nights a week. On the weekends, I was usually trying to catch up on academic work I did not have time for during the week and so could only go to the post erratically. Once this pattern became clear, his interest rapidly waned. I would become more engaged with the *Legion* later, when I was working in "the City" and my evenings were free; even working as a volunteer at the big bingo games which the post sponsored. I have never forgotten the intensity with which the bingo *habitues,* primarily women, approached the game, some playing eight or ten cards at a time, with a passionate commitment which banished all sense of courtesy or even civility. Nor have I forgotten the density of the smoke which filled the hall. Even as a three pack a day man, I was stunned by just the sheer visibility of the smoke hanging in the air like a London fog in a Sherlock Holmes novel.

My next encounter with a potential new circle once again came from an Iona College bulletin board and was to be much more successful than my small CNR sortie. In the 1950s, the American Catholic church was quite concerned about what was then termed a "mixed marriage." As then understood, a mixed marriage was one between a Roman Catholic and a partner of a different religious denomination. As the ethnic segregation of the Catholic Irish, Italians, Slavs, etc., was breaking down with moves to suburban living, as a result of post-World War II prosperity, young Catholic men and women were, as they had never been before, finding themselves in homes and jobs and social situations which placed them cheek by jowl with religious "others." The fears of the Catholic hierarchy about loss of faith or loss of identity were, interestingly, generally mirrored in the period by Jewish religious and social leaders, who displayed many of the same anxieties, and often suggested similar palliatives or solutions. One such solution had been embodied in the CNR Tea Dance goal: "let's provide social occasions where the young men and women involved will be, at least primarily, composed of Roman Catholics." It was in that context that I noted a notice an Iona bulletin board saying that the nearby (a couple of blocks up the hill) Holy Family Church, had established a club (the Martin Club) for unmarried Catholics in their twenties and thirties. Well, I was twenty, and I did want to meet young women, so I noted the days and times of their meetings/socials and decided, once again, to attempt to expand my circle of acquaintances.

Soon after, on one of the appointed evenings, surely a Friday or a Saturday, dressed (as was the norm) in jacket and tie, I presented myself at

Holy Family Church. A group of twenty to thirty, with a roughly equal number of men and women, assembled. Dancing and general conversation and some discrete flirting ensued, and the time passed rapidly and cheerfully, and, as I headed back down North Ave., I realized that I had met some congenial people (more men than women), enjoyed myself and decided that I would certainly return in the near future. The Martin Club would, in fact, outside Iona, become the core of my social life for the next couple of years until; as its members paired off, it sort of married itself out of existence. In the meantime the members, there were probably nearly sixty of us from start to finish, met, talked, dated one another, played softball, had parties and picnics until, in one way or another, we moved on. In the way of voluntary associations, if we totaled fifty or sixty, the bulk of the work, whether planning and organization or the basic physical efforts of setting up halls, decorating, etc., fell to the lot of a much smaller group. I would, happily, join that effort and enjoyed rewarding friendships and many pleasant activities. Naturally enough, we formed close social bonds and we thought of ourselves, and called ourselves, *The Faithful Seventeen.*

A few words about the Faithful Seventeen might be appropriate. We ranged from twenty (I think I was, as always, still the youngest) to our late twenties. We were from the nature of our association, all Catholic and all single. Ethnically we were Irish and Italian, German and Slavic, with an odd Anglo or two, but all of European background. Some of us were idealistic, some, at least ostensibly, cynical and at least one rather naive.

Among us there was a very blond and very attractive young woman, who we shall call Marilyn, because she bore a resemblance to Miss Monroe. She once reduced a roomful of us to tears of laughter with what was in fact a quite scary true story. Told in a frank and straightforward manner, but redolent with innocence, she explained to us that somehow she had managed to get on Connecticut's Merritt Parkway (a limited access highway) going the wrong way. As Marilyn told the story, she was at first pleased because "all of the drivers seemed so friendly. They were all waving and honking…."

Another member, the fellow we called Jimmy LaFrere was, like me, a Korean War vet, though he had been an officer and seen combat as an artillery forward observer. Jimmy would tell us of a dark and lonely night when his position was in front of our lines and exposed. Stuck in a valley, he had a genuine reason to fear enemy patrols. After hearing repeated sounds of stealthy motion near his position, he called in a fire mission. The guns roared. When the sun came up, there were no signs of enemy casualties but, as Jimmy was wont to say, there was "the deadest damn deer anyone will ever see." Jimmy would marry Margaret Mary, and, even in the early days, he would serenade her, in a pleasant enough baritone, with songs from *My Fair Lady*. We did such things in those days.

In the 1950s, if there was any kind of Catholic group or association, it almost certainly had a moderator, and he was, equally surely, a priest. In the case of the Martin Club, that was Father John Leibfred, a priest assigned to Holy Family church. Holy Family was a very large church and parish. In addition to the Monsignor who was the pastor, there were at least three curates (including Fr. Leibfred) as well as a second Monsignor who lived in the rectory but worked in New York City in an administrative capacity for the Archdiocese of New York.[1]

Father John Leibfred was a very pleasant, if somewhat taciturn, man who attended our events with considerable regularity, often offered good advice (though rarely without solicitation) and who possessed an admirable sense of duty. In those days, with many priests available in a parish, they usually operated a night duty roster. That meant that each night of the week, a priest was "on call" to respond to calls for accidents, sickness or sudden death throughout the night. It was well known that when Fr. Leibfred "had the duty," he stayed up all night. He may have dozed sitting up, but if a call

---

[1] It might be well to note here that diocesan priests (sometimes called secular priests) who worked in the parishes and reported to the bishop of the diocese, were normally addressed by their title and surname (Good morning, Father Smith). Priests who were members of religious orders, particularly the Franciscans, who would loom so large in my life, were then customarily addressed by title and Christian name or name in religion (so, my Timon history teacher, Father Arnold Brown, in greeting or conversation was simply, Father Arnold.) The distinction, while it still persists, rather faded in the 1970s and 80s and the secular form became dominant.

came, he was fully dressed and ready to respond. If he was needed, he wanted no delays – he would be ready to go in an instant.

He was a genuine intellectual and, when you could get him to open up, a splendid conversationalist and *raconteur.* About twenty years older than we were, he still fit among us very well. He was also very devout. He was, we discovered over time, also an exorcist for the Archdiocese of New York. The church chooses her exorcists based on the perceived depth of their Christianity and their maturity. He was once persuaded, in a small group, to briefly talk about his experiences as an exorcist. Suffice it to say that those of us who were in that group and later read Blatty's, *The Exorcist*, or saw the film, were perhaps not as shocked as many of our contemporaries. Fr. Leibfred was a happy, confident, thoughtful, and, I believe, a genuinely holy man.

Sometime in November of 1955 I noticed two girls coming into the church hall. One was quite tall, perhaps an inch or so taller than I was. The other was a more conventional height, perhaps 5'3" or 5'4". The first was a brunette, the second, a strawberry blond. Let's call the taller girl Sharon. The strawberry blond was Dorothy. During the evening, I struck up a conversation with them and found them to be good company. It turned out that they had both graduated from college that June. They had gone to high school together and, it seemed, had vied with one another for the various academic prizes, medals, etc., at graduation. Shortly thereafter, I made a date with Sharon and we went out two or three times. A few weeks later, in late January of 1956, at a Martin Club social, I found myself involved in a lengthy conversation with Dorothy. When the party ended, I asked her if she would allow me to walk her home. Since she lived only a few blocks from the church, my lack of an automobile was no impediment. The evening had been exceptionally pleasant, so the next day, I called and asked her to go out with me the following Friday evening. She said she was busy. I then asked her to go out the following Saturday. Once again, she regretted her unavailability. I now found myself in a classic male dilemma. I had just been rejected twice in a row. If she simply did not wish to see me, I did not wish to force myself upon her. My mind quickly rationalized that we certainly had enjoyed one another's company and that I was already on the phone. I'm sure, also that somewhere I could hear my mother's voice repeating an old Irish adage, "You might as well be hung for [stealing] a sheep as a lamb." So, I asked, perhaps with a slight note of doubt in my voice, "what about next weekend?" As it turned out, that weekend was free, and we made our first date. I was pleased but certainly not conscious of the fact that I had just begun what was to be the most important relationship in my life.

It was the mid-1950s and we of the Martin Club fit virtually all the stereotypes. As specified above, we were all Caucasian, all middle-class, all Catholics and we all adhered to stereotypical gender roles. If we were going to have a dance, the men moved the tables and the women decorated. (I might mention that Holy Family had two venues for dances, the classic church basement and a really delightful rooftop, piazza-like space which, on a summer night was quite lovely.) We all also dressed appropriately; girls wore dresses or skirts and blouses (interestingly, by now the very word blouse seems to have disappeared from the language) and guys wore shirts and ties. I don't think I remember any young women in slacks except at outdoor functions like picnics or softball games. At softball games, men played and women watched. We were, indeed, quite a bit like a fictional New Rochelle resident of the era, Dick Van Dyke's Rob Petrie.

We also formed the usual smaller groupings which ranged from the Faithful Seventeen to groups of two or three. So, for example, I became quite close to a native of New Rochelle who tended to introduce himself as Vincent Joseph Michael Scully. Vince was a Navy veteran who was also an Iona man. He was one of the most cheerful and decent men I have ever met. He was a font of humor, always willing to laugh at himself and always ready to lend a hand. He was the classic "give you the shirt off his back" kind of guy. Dick Bocek, an Army veteran, of Czech descent who always seemed older than the rest of us was also a close companion. If Vince was the source of good humor and fun, Dick was the keystone of good sense and clear thinking. Both would become close companions and both would be members of my wedding party. It was Dick, who was the First Sergeant of an Army Reserve Military Police Company in Long Island City, who persuaded me to join the active reserves briefly. He needed some help, specifically, an NCO to act as a sort of Field First Sergeant when the company went to summer camp. It was this experience which enabled me to recover my status as an NCO which, for some not very clear reason, seemed important to me. There were of course many others: the Carlin brothers, Frank Toner, Steve H. and on and on. Whether it was a quick beer or a cup of coffee someplace or a longer session (I do remember one at the *American Legion* when one of my friends had recently been "unlucky in love" and we engaged one another on a variety of topics from intense to inane until his mood lightened.) Whether because I met Dorothy early and quickly became focused on her, I am not sure, but I formed no serious bonds with any of the other girls. I was friendly with them all, worked well with them, and enjoyed their company, but I was never particularly close to any.

Meanwhile, down the hill and across North Avenue, my academic life began and raced forward. The courses I was taking were those normally taken by freshmen majoring in the liberal arts. That meant six courses; five were three credits each and fulfilled core course requirements or those required by one's major. Each semester we were also required to take a two credit course in religion, which ranged from Church History to the Christian Family and Fundamentals of Sacred Theology. Thus it was anticipated that, at graduation each student would present 120 credits plus sixteen in religion. I greatly enjoyed most of my coursework. The introductory courses in English and History were well organized and presented. I found my introductory Philosophy course in Logic to be very interesting and easily manageable. The Religion course in Moral Law was less well presented but moderately interesting. The introductory math course I found very dull and, as a result, difficult. My elementary French course was taught by an excellent teacher, Dr. Mondelli, whose focus was on spoken rather than written French. He was a man I genuinely liked. Unfortunately, I hated the very thought of the public pronunciation of French. Translation and the written word were , dare I say, much closer to my *métier.* The result was, overall satisfactory but not much more. (I have never understood why I had decided to opt for French rather than continue with my high school choice, Spanish. Though it was clear that French was considered academically more respectable.)

As the fall term came to an end, my focus was forced to change. Iona, the Martin Club and *Howard Johnson's* had nicely filled my days and evenings and I was developing a genuine circle of friends and acquaintances in each of those areas. Suddenly, however, a new reality intruded itself. My father had become ill; he had even been hospitalized. With his salary no longer available, our economic circumstances had to be addressed. The monies I generated from the GI Bill and from *Howard Johnson's* clearly would not be adequate to go to college, pay the rent and put food on the table. A rather full and somewhat anxious review of the situation, as well as possible solutions, short of a gigantic visitation from the tooth fairy, suggested only one possibility. I would have to withdraw from Iona, at least temporarily, and find a job. Mentally, I assured myself that it would just be long enough to tide us over.

Not the least painful part of this decision lay in the fact that I am awful at job hunting. The mechanics, as they then were, were simple enough. First, get hold of the local newspaper (*The New Rochelle Standard Star*) and several New York City papers and read the want ads. (One of the glories of Imperial New York in those days was the depth and breadth of newspaper coverage. There were more than seven newspapers published in NYC at that time. They ranged from tabloids like the *News and Mirror* to more serious papers like the *Times* and *the Herald Tribune.* Most had some virtues. The *Post* for example was a bad paper but had wonderful columnists. *My* papers were the *Herald Tribune* and the *New York World Telegram and Sun.*) The job hunting problem for me lay not in application forms but in writing supporting letters and in interviews. I am, and always have been highly articulate and more than marginally persuasive. But I have never been good at "selling me." I find it painfully embarrassing to have to say good things about myself. Fortunately, with little direct work experience, the jobs for which I applied were low enough on the food chain that those parts of the process proved minimal. Rather quickly, I found a job in "the City," with the *Chase Manhattan Bank*. I started down in the Wall Street area (18 Pine) but quite quickly found myself assigned to mid-town, the Graybar Building Branch, which was cheek by jowl with Grand Central Terminal. Since my commute from New Rochelle terminated there, it proved a real convenience. I was making about $47.00 a week and the $18.00 a month cost for a commuter's ticket represented a significant expense. Nonetheless, the job with *Chase* solved the immediate economic problem. As it turned out, I would work for *Chase* from January of 1956 until I returned to Iona at the start of the fall term, 1956. After that, it would be part-time work again until I was hired for my first teaching appointment in September of 1960. Prior to that, I would work for *Western Union* and the Iona College library. I briefly delivered cases of *Pepsi* and other sodas from a truck, mostly in the Bronx. At two Christmas seasons, I gladly found work with the U.S. Post Office, which paid exceptionally well. I also worked nights in New Rochelle for a bank clearing house where we used machines to sort checks and send them to the bank they were drawn on and, one summer, I directed a summer camp. The Iona Library job was by far the steadiest, lasting for two years.

I had now become a "check desk clerk" in the bookkeeping department of *Chase*. Our work was not done on the floor of the bank, but upstairs, out of sight. A very large room contained something like a dozen bookkeepers, perhaps a half-dozen check desk clerks and supervisory personnel. The bookkeepers tracked all bank transactions. That is, if you wrote a check, they deducted the amount from your account. If you deposited a check or some other financial instrument, they added that amount to your account. Check desk clerks performed a number of functions including visually checking the authenticity of personal signatures. If necessary, they compared the signature in question to that on file. They also canceled checks.

Chase at that time canceled checks by inserting them in a machine which perforated the check so it clearly was no longer valid. Our supervisor, colloquially called "Dutch," used to regale us with stories of "the old days." When he came back from World War II, he told us, checks were cancelled by machine with red ink. When we complained of the tedium of check canceling, he would tell us how that ink would flare out and "ruin a shirt" every day you canceled checks.

The clerks also prepared debits and credits for posting and then delivered them to the bookkeepers. If, at the end of the day, one or more bookkeepers failed to "prove" (that is, one or more accounts did not balance to the penny), then the clerks would assist in the search for the error. Sometimes, tellers would be brought up from the main floor to assist. At that time, if such corrective measures were necessary, you worked for free for the first hour after normal closing, because a very generous *Chase Manhattan* had given you an hour for lunch and, *the least you could do was to occasionally compensate the bank.* After the first hour, you went on overtime and, after six, you were also entitled to "supper money."

If a bookkeeper "showed" (failed to prove) then it was all hands on deck, at least until six. As six approached (and with it the possibility of overtime and supper money), it was usually found that a smaller group was adequate to continue the quest. Of course, not infrequently, the problem might have been due to a badly written number on a check, or the accidental transposition of a number or a check or credit overlooked. I can remember searches going on until eight or nine o'clock for less than a dollar. Only once did it prove impossible to find the error.

I worked with an interesting and, on the whole, very pleasant group of people. "Dutch," our overall supervisor was a World War II veteran, and, in the better sense of the phrase, a real "company man." His trust in and loyalty to the company was nearly absolute. Nevertheless, he was never anything other than courteous and friendly to his subordinates. By way of illustrating the former, he once told me that on his first major holiday, back from the war, when there was a major problem, he slept over in a hotel room so that he could continue to work on the problem early the next morning. When a couple of us suggested that we would have chosen a different course, Dutch just smiled and moved along. He was a good man to work for who easily won respect and even affection from people whose work ethic was different from his own. I also affectionately remember a wonderful teller, called Thomasine, whom we all loved. If someone "showed," even if she was not involved she would, almost invariably, come upstairs after she had closed out her accounts, to lend a hand. If the problem was persistent, she would even, on occasion, sign out at six (that supper money issue) and keep on working to help us out. One result of her attitude versus that of the bank would prove ironic. Her husband was in the Army, stationed in Germany. Then he came home. The night his troop ship was due into Hoboken there was a major problem and *Chase* asked Thomasina to stay and help out. She said that she was sorry but that husband's ship was due in and she intended to meet it. By this time it was past midsummer, and a few weeks later we were called in individually to discuss out personal efficiency reports. To everyone's surprise (and some anger) we found out that Thomasina had been deemed "uncooperative." The child was the very soul of cooperation. None of us knew what to do. My own report came a day or two later. By now my father had recovered, and I was preparing to return to Iona. I was pleased that my own evaluation was virtually glowing and that I was being promised a raise of about three dollars a week, which by the standards of the day (and of *Chase*) was quite generous. I seized my opportunity. There are few times in life when we can, simultaneously, do what we know to be right, vent, and I suppose "posture" is the right word, with impunity. They did not know that I was about to return to college. I outlined for them Thomasina's role and the respect in which her colleagues held her. I suggested that their rating system needed work, I gave them two weeks' notice and I told them, politely though probably somewhat pompously as well, what I thought of what I saw as a miscarriage of justice. I probably did no good, but I felt better and certainly never had any reason to change my opinion. And so I prepared to return to college.

During the Chase interval, I had come to know, and like Dorothy (Dorothy Louise Schiller) very much. We moved, fairly rapidly, from dating to what would then have been called "going steady." By midsummer, in Martin Club circles, no one spoke of Tom or of Dorothy, the usage was "Tom and Dorothy" or "Dottie and Tom." In large degree, this had happened, on my part almost unconsciously. In fact, for a while, in early summer, I was dating Dorothy and one of the bookkeepers at Chase, called Mary Dealy. (My feminine social circle had certainly expanded rapidly since my discharge.) One evening, I had taken Mary out to dinner and at the end of what I had thought to be a pleasant and uneventful night, she rather abruptly said to me, "I think you ought to marry Dorothy." Since, to my knowledge she didn't know anything about Dorothy, I was taken aback and stumbled over something like "how did you know about Dorothy?" To which she replied, "Because you've been calling me Dorothy all night!" I felt foolish and I realized that I had been terribly unkind. I still think so.

My employment with *Chase* in "the City" meant that, in addition to dating, Dot and I also had a chance for an additional forty-five minutes or so together while we commuted into work. She was then working for *Eastman Chemical Products*, on Madison Avenue while I was at Grand Central. On rare occasions we also met for lunch where I was to discover that when a young woman ordered a "jelly omelet" – there actually was such a thing! Our schedules made it impossible to synchronize the ride home. We had a great deal in common. We were both practicing Roman Catholics and products of parochial elementary and high schools, she in metropolitan New York, I, Upstate. She, by virtue of skipping a grade, had already graduated from Marywood College (now Marywood U.) in Scranton, Pa., where she had been awarded a scholarship. She had planned to teach, but as a college senior, after practice teaching, she discovered that teaching was not her cup of tea. As a result, as was then said, "She went to business." We had similar, somewhat retro, tastes in music: more "big band" than the then incoming rock and roll. Nor had it escaped my attention that she was attractive and possessed of a very nice figure. The Martin Club, with its church dances,

159

picnics and softball games, suited us well, and its merry band of like-minded men and women, with the occasional house party and the odd trip to Greenwich Village for an evening, was also a good fit.

We began to talk more seriously and to, more or less automatically, take one another into account in our planning. At one point in this period, when I was unsure when, if ever, I could get back to college, I considered re-enlisting and perhaps seeking a commission. Out for a walk, Dorothy reminded me of my hopes and aspirations with regard to becoming a professor of history. There was a time, too, when I went to Washington, DC, to interview with the National Security Agency, where my Army experience had direct relevance. The interview went well, and I was reasonably assured that the job was available to me. On the bus ride back, however, I realized that if I took it, I would need, at least in the short run, to be in the Washington area for training and orientation. On reflection, I decided that I did not want to be separated from Dorothy for any length of time. I dropped further consideration of a career with the NSA. It was becoming increasingly clear to me that I was in love with this modest and retiring young woman and that there was every likelihood that my feelings were reciprocated.

From a practical point of view, that kind of thinking was insane. I had just turned twenty-one. The 1956 election would be my first opportunity to vote. I had completed one semester of college. I was, with Dorothy's encouragement, walking away from steady job. She had graduated from college only a year earlier, gotten her first job and just turned twenty-two. In short, we had nothing, other than a romantic attachment for one another and a confidence in the (and our) future based far more on faith than reality. Thus it was that we decided to marry.

So, in September, 1956, I returned to Iona, to part-time employment and to thoughts and plans of academic work and the thoughts of marrying this lovely girl. I had sought and found employment, one town over, in Mount Vernon, NY, with the *Western Union Telegraph Company*. (A condition of employment was membership in the telegrapher's union. I am not sure how much return on investment I received during my employment, but in later years I often found it amusing in discussions in faculty lounges to be able to note during political arguments that I was the only one in the room who had ever carried a union card.) To summarize the 1956-57 academic year, I went to class, I went to work, I studied, I lost a good deal of sleep courting the woman I loved and I recorded the two worst academic semesters of my life. During the first semester of my years at Iona, my Grade Point Average (GPA) was about 3.3. In the fall and spring terms of 1956-57, my GPA was 2.5 and 2.4.

The *Western Union* office was in Mount Vernon, not far from New Rochelle. I would leave my last class, grab a bus and head to the office. I worked until 9:00 p.m. Dorothy would often borrow her family's car and come to Mount Vernon and go to the movies. She would then pick me up and we would go for coffee, or just to her house, and talk for an hour or so. I would then walk home, about another 45 minutes. I then got a modicum of sleep, arose and faced the new day. I headed for Iona, where I was taking six courses for 17 credits in the fall and seven courses and 19 credits in the spring. I was aware, needing to get into a decent University for graduate study, that my grades were reason for alarm. But, I couldn't cut back on work or course-work, and I **wouldn't** cut back on the limited time I had with Dottie. And so, seeing no alternative, I, as our British cousins say, "muddled through."

My career as an unmarried undergraduate encompassed less than two years, from Sept. 1955 until June of 1957. My strengths were the liberal arts, my weaknesses in mathematics and, to a degree, French. The Iona faculty was, to the best of my memory, all male at that time, with a mixture of perhaps 66/33 lay and clerical. There were two women, both librarians on the professional staff. The strength of the faculty lay in teaching rather than research and, on the whole, they were serious, hardworking and adept at that function. Certainly, I learned a great deal, not only formally, in subject matter instruction, but also by example. So, by observation I learned how (and how not) to approach students and to teach them. I can still remember Professor Brophy, in English Lit class telling us, "I do not have a right to demand that you agree with me. I do have a right to demand indications that you have heard me." I tried to adhere to that model throughout my career. Dr. Paul Peeters, who wrote an interesting book in those years, entitled *Massive Retaliation: The Policy and Its Critics*, taught my first history course. I chose the Roman Army on the march as my term paper topic: how did that army move, what did it carry, what were its security concerns, how did it encamp, etc.? Peeters had required that once your topic had been approved, you were to carry out your research, organize the paper and stipulate your conclusions and then schedule a conference with him before you began to write. I enjoyed the preparation, including a number of hours in the vast reading room of the main branch of the NYC public library, and, when ready, arranged a meeting.

After about twenty minutes or so of reading and discussion, followed by a few questions about the bibliography, he asked for my conclusions. He then announced that he was satisfied. I began to leave and said something about a first draft. He told me that I had misunderstood his intent. I had satisfied the course requirement. I was to be awarded a grade of A for the paper, and it need not be written. I never adopted this process because I thought the writing too important a part of the exercise, but I did see a good deal of sense in it. In my adaptation, I would require all of my students to schedule a conference, at least to gain approval for their topics and to be sure they understood the parameters of their work. Peeters, a Belgian by birth, had taken his doctorate at Louvain and had come to the U.S. after World War II. Based on remarks he made, in and out of class, his associations with American college students had produced a form of culture shock. The result was a disdain, verging upon contempt, which formed an important part of his public persona. That characteristic played a part in our next personal interaction, which was much less pleasant. In a lecture class, he called on one of my classmates and a fellow veteran, called Brooks. In what was almost a chant, he intoned, "We will call on Mr. Brooks, rippling, bubbling, babbling Brooks." Brooks, who was an exceptionally hardworking man, but who was not the most articulate member of our class, was virtually stunned into silence. Dr. Peeters then said, "We will call on Mr. Kelly." Somewhat stunned myself, and very angry, I replied "No!" He then said, "You do not know the answer?" I, in full blown arrogance, responded, "We both know that I know the answer, but I will not give it to you." He moved on with his lecture and, to give him his due, though I took several other classes with him, he never mentioned the exchange nor did he ever display any ill will toward me. I suspect that, given more time to think, my response might have been less direct, though I never dreamed of regretting it.

In many American colleges in the post-World War II era, there were numerous emigres who lent sophistication, sadness and sometimes humor to the campus. At Iona, in the History Department, besides Dr. Peeters, there was Dr. Bohdan Chudoba. A Czech, he had one book burned by the Nazis and another destroyed on the press by the Communists. He had, the story went, skied out of Czechoslovakia to freedom and, like Dr. Peeters, managed to get to the U.S. where, he too, was amazed by the very different life he found in the American "groves of academe." He never reconciled himself to the clerical and administrative burdens placed on him by the administration. At one point I was in a very large lecture session (perhaps 55 students) he was teaching. It included ten or twelve "student brothers" – young men who aspired to become Irish Christian Brothers and were working on their bachelor's degree while preparing for their religious lives.

At this time, probably prodded by the Veteran's Administration (seeking to be sure that folks on the GI Bill were actually going to class), the college administration sent the faculty rather draconic memos about taking roll. Chudoba rarely if ever did a roll call. On this particular day he did. He announced that when your name was called, you should come to his desk and present your student ID. His intent was clearly to embarrass the administration, but he was about to get a bonus. When he reached the first student brother it was made evident, that they had not been provided with student ID cards. In a dramatic flurry, the rather shocked student brother was made to stand against the back wall of the class. When roll call was finished, he had been joined by all of the other brothers in the class. By this time also, about 45 minutes of a 50 minute academic hour had passed. But roll call was finished. Chudoba, normally the least dramatic of men, now drew himself up into a figure of (make-believe) anger, shouted that now we all knew where the source of the absentee problem could be found and ordered the brothers collectively to "Report yourselves to the dean at once." To the best of my knowledge, he never took roll again. Nor, I suspect, was he ever asked again.

Chudoba had an excellent book on Charles V and the Hapsburg Empire to his credit and during my time published an interesting book with the "modest" title of *The Meaning of Civilization*. His accent was quite a bit thicker than Peeters', and he had a wicked, if usually hidden, sense of humor. Once, when we were waiting for the start of a final examination, a student called Jack Penny, known to all to be shameless in currying favor, asked Dr. Chudoba if he had finished correcting the term papers for the course because he (Jack) was very interested in the evaluation of his work. Chudoba responded, "Ah, Mr. Penny, your paper was so interesting that I gave it to my grandmother to read, and she is not yet finished."

Brother Mark Hunt taught Religion and was the sexton for Iona's chapel. He was a patient and long suffering instructor who really loved his students, though he was rarely able to galvanize them into academic action. His reputation as a "good grader" seemed to insulate his audience from any substantial effort. He did, on at least one occasion, try to suggest that there was a sterner self, when he told a class, "I had to fail a boy once. He gave me heresy on a final exam." One day, leaving the chapel, I offered a compliment on how beautifully the chapel (a quite unprepossessing structure) was kept. He paused, leaned toward me and, in a very low, confidential voice, told me, "I get everything from an Episcopal supply house." I do think faculties *qua* faculties were much more interesting and colorful then than they have since become. On another occasion, I had been asked to assist a devout Episcopalian, a neighbor of Dorothy's parents, on a project in which he hoped to prove the validity of Anglican Orders. That is, to prove that the Bishops of the Anglican Church had a proper place in the Apostolic

Succession of bishops. Unsure of where this might lead, I spoke to Brother Hunt who dealt with the problem expeditiously: "Do you plan to lie or deceive in the conclusion of the research"?" he asked. "No," I replied. "Well then," said Brother Mark, "Augustine tells us, 'Where there is truth, there is the Holy Ghost.'"

As veterans, we often chafed at college regulations. We were, for example, required to attend classes wearing a jacket and tie. This annoyed us so, that, as sophomores, we requested a meeting with the college president and asked that the college at least consider a more liberal dress code. I had been selected as one of the spokesmen. The good brother heard us out, with courtesy and forbearance. He listened with apparent attention to our modest list of reasons in support of a change. Then, with exquisite courtesy, denied our request and showed us out. I was not then to know how many times in the future college administrators would find it necessary, or at least pleasant, to show me the door.

Dr. Mondelli continued to be a delightful man and excellent instructor whose emphasis on spoken French represented the wave of the future. My psyche, or maybe just my ego, continued to swim against the tide, which barely got me through the first six credits of my language requirement. Happily, the next six credits were at the hands of less talented but more traditional instructors, who favored the older style of reading and written translation. As a result, while I would never earn honors in French, my grades improved markedly. In math, I "came a cropper." Having done reasonably well in the first three math credits, I confronted the next three as I returned to college. Iona was, at this time, quite crowded and an elderly brother had been brought out of retirement to teach. I was assigned to his class. I don't think that I ever understood, for a moment, what he was doing. He was pleasant and offered tutorial assistance, which I pursued. We met two or three times a week for an hour. He instructed us to begin an equation and take it as far as we could – then he would be along to help. Since something approaching half or more of the class was present, perhaps his intentions were unrealizable. Day after day, I would present myself, begin the

165

equation and wait. Help literally never arrived. By midterm time, when I still had not had one minute's worth of assistance, I stopped attending. That semester, in that course, I received the only failing grade of my life. My mother, I am sure, would have told me, "Tom, it's good for your humility," and she probably would have been right. On the other hand, it was not good for my ego (or my GPA) – but then, ego, unlike humility is not a virtue. That stubborn ego, though, does require me, even at this distance in time, to point out that the following semester, with a different instructor, rumored to have worked on the Manhattan Project, I aced the course, and completed my math requirement. I also learned something about assisting students. Regardless of the amount of time involved, tutorials are defined as one on one because they need to be one on one. The amount of time is less significant than understanding where the student lags and why.

I had discovered quite early that the then normal "cut" policy system in college was very much to my liking. Most instructors allowed six cuts in a three credit course meeting three days a week. Outside courses which gave me academic difficulty, I was always full cut in every course. That is, I absented myself from class the maximum number of times allowed without penalty. Usually, I was "full cut" by midterms. Indeed, I remember after we were married Dorothy being very worried about my use of cuts. "What will you do if you get sick?" was her reasonable query – to which she usually got some dismissive mumbled response. In the event, it never came to that. There was one near disaster, not from excessive cuts, but from timing. I was deeply involved in a coffee klatch discussion in the college cafeteria, perhaps about Fidel Castro in the hills in Cuba, when I realized that it was time for Mr. Brophy's English class. I decided I would take a cut and continue the discussion. An hour later, one of the members of the class came in and asked me where I had been. "I took a cut," I said. He looked at me like I had two heads and said, "Today was the midterm." I was suddenly, deeply, anxious. I had thought the midterm was the following class day. After a few minutes thought, I decided that honesty was not only the best policy, it was the only policy at my command. I went immediately to Mr. Brophy's office.

Once there, I told him exactly what had happened and why and, to lend some credence to my position, offered, then and there, to sit for the test, should he be kind enough to provide that latitude. As it turned out, after making me sweat for a day or two, he did allow me a makeup exam. Other than that, I never did have a problem with cuts and went on my way, unrepentant, and full cut.

In my sophomore year I took one course each term in American History with the intention of fulfilling that portion of the requirement for the major. My long term goal remained teaching American History in college. I had, however, decided that, though American was my first love, I would load up on European and other histories during my time at Iona in order to develop breadth. My thinking was influenced by the notion that in my proposed graduate school program I would be required to take many courses in American History. By stressing European History at Iona, I would be better prepared for comprehensive exams in graduate school. Experience would indicate that it did work. Later, at Fordham University, I took only one or two courses in European History prior to my Master's comprehensive examination and did well anyway. Immediately, I bolstered my U.S. background by taking courses at Iona in American Literature, Art and Political Science. I have contended, from that day to this, that no matter how diligently one studied, nor how deep his research, if he did not have a grasp of the literature and art of the culture and the period, he could not really know or understand its history. The reverse is also true. Such cultural knowledge enables the scholar to capture the thought of the period, and of the people. History, in its turn, provides clues which provide a deeper understanding of the art and literature.

My routine in the 1956-57 academic year was to attend my classes each weekday for a period of three to four hours, with time for lunch. After class, I caught a bus to Mount Vernon (perhaps 20-30 minutes not including waiting time). There, I reported to *Western Union* for work. My usual stint was about five hours, during which I was primarily engaged in taking telegrams on the phone and sending them on to their destination via teletype. Despite its origins and formal name, by this time, there was no telegraphy used by *Western Union*. In those distant days the great ocean liners still sailed for Europe from the port of New York and, frequently, our wires were *bon voyage* messages addressed to outbound passengers. I remember a particular instance, when a man was cutting it fine – really too close to sailing time to guarantee delivery but seeking assurance that it was delivered. At that moment, we were not too busy and so I followed up for him. Unlikely as it was, I was able to guarantee it had been delivered. Several days later, a package arrived at the office for me. It turned out that he was a major official in a pharmaceutical company and I became the recipient of a very long term supply of analgesics, antiseptics and antacids. Perhaps the most interesting telegraphic message I ever took involved an old acquaintance. As I was taking the message, I became increasingly sure that I knew the voice – though I could not place it. When I asked for the signature, it was George Edmund Badger, my old platoon sergeant from basic training. We exchanged pleasantries, talked about coincidences and moved on.

There was also a large volume of business traffic, but by the time I usually arrived, that was nearly always just about finished. By closing time, I had been on the move for eleven hours or more. If I was lucky, Dorothy had borrowed her father's car, come to Mount Vernon and gone to the movies. If so, she would pick me up, and we would drive back to New Rochelle for that cup of coffee or to her house for conversation and perhaps a bit of necking. After that came the walk back home. By now my day was between twelve and fourteen hours long and without an opportunity to crack a book, or review any lecture notes. Academic work was pretty well reserved for weekends, in between Martin Club activities, with and without Dorothy, and the time necessary for us to further contemplate our feelings for one another. I should certainly point out here that Dorothy was always anxious to help me in any way she could. Indeed, from September 1956 on, it was she who saved me many hours and much frustration, by typing all my term papers – including the then infuriating problems of erasures and corrections, not only of originals but also the one or more carbon copies which were then requisite and the correction of which required far more patience than I had ever possessed.

For my part, between dates and dances and conventional courtship rituals, I was convinced that she was the woman with whom I wished to spend the rest of my life. I managed to accumulate a small amount of money, and one of my classmates let drop the fact that his uncle was, in a small way, in the wholesale jewelry business. Shortly thereafter, I ended up somewhere around Pine St. in lower Manhattan handing over my small hoard and asking that the stone, no matter how small, be flawless and the setting white gold. About a month later, on a lovely autumn Saturday, in downtown New Rochelle, we stopped in my parish church, Blessed Sacrament, for what Catholics call "a visit." That is just what it sounds like; there is no ritual or ceremony, one just stops in the church, says a prayer and leaves. In those pre-Vatican II days, when women were required to have a head covering in church, most Catholic women and girls carried a small piece of lace or a scarf or *babushka*, to place on their heads, if necessary. Dottie was not, I think, surprised that I was asking her to marry me, nor was I when she accepted. I think both of us were very sure and I, at least, was very happy.

Leaving church, we went across the street to a nearby *Mayflower Doughnut Shop* for a cup of coffee. To this day, I remember a poster there, perhaps a sort of *mantra* or inane motto. It said:

As you go through life, brother
Whatever may be your goal
Keep your eye upon the doughnut
And not upon the hole.

For some reason, that day, it amused me inordinately.

We decided to marry at the end of the following summer, on August 31, 1957. Other than researching what portion of the wedding the groom was expected to pay for, anything else, as Dorothy's mother reminded me, fell under the purview of the bride (and her mother). Loretta and George,

Dot's Mom and Dad, were wonderful people and I often wonder how they felt with their daughter about to join her life to an impecunious undergraduate with no visible prospect of success. Whatever trepidations they may have had were well hidden. For that, as well as for their daughter, I have always been grateful.

My own family, while they may have considered the decision to marry as imprudent, had no doubts about the girl. The "Kane girls" loved Dorothy almost from the moment they met her and considered me "thrice blest." Once the date for the wedding was set, a wedding shower was scheduled. Since the clan was to gather at Kitty's home in Rutherford, and it was family only, males were permitted to attend. It had a "domestic" theme, so the gifts were highly utilitarian. That was of course thoroughly Kane – if a new household was to be set up, it would need unglamorous things, such as measuring cups and buckets for mops (both of which we still have).

All were properly festooned with various ribbons and other festive touches. Dorothy was properly surprised; I had told her we were going to a family dinner. She was also gratified, I think, by the complete sense of belonging which surrounded her. My father also thought well of her and congratulated me on having persuaded her to marry me. Since he was, once again, "on the outs" with his brother and sisters, the Norwalk Kellys, their introduction to Dottie would come later.

My aunts were not entirely satisfied with Dorothy's shower. There was also the fact that my mother had been dead now for almost seven years, during which none of the "Kane girls" had been able to properly supervise me. I think there was a fear that I should arrive in the bridal chamber in a state unsuitable for a Kane. In any event, and for whatever reason, I was presented with what I have always thought of as "Tom's Trousseau." There were two pairs of pajamas, slippers, and a very nice, lightweight flannel robe. There may have been more attire, but that is what I remember, and so, I suspect, my aunts rested assured that my new bride would not be scandalized by her husband's bedroom attire. The complete package also included two leather suitcases with my initials inscribed.

I continued through the spring term with my academic, social, economic and romantic activities. In general, I was quite happy, though usually quite tired. I had also found time to dabble in undergraduate politics; perhaps a hangover from our crusade against the dress code. Anyway, our group thought that the large group of veterans ought to be represented on the student council. I perceived myself as a sort of behind-the-scenes figure, and the group persuaded one of our cohort, I think it may have been John DeMartino, to accept nomination. John was a thoughtful and serious man, who presented a formidable figure. He was handsome, always impeccably dressed (frequently more so than the faculty) and very articulate. Unfortunately for the cause (though perhaps fortunately for my already strained GPA) we failed to win. As it was, I staggered through the term with a GPA of only 2.4, a full point lower than my first semester. I had started trying to catch up for the semester I had lost, by carrying an extra course that spring but, as we have seen, that did not go well. In the summer of 1957, I took three credits in philosophy, and, rather optimistically, I had registered for twenty-one credits in the fall term of 1957.

The summer passed somewhat slowly, though the Philosophy course aided my GPA. As the wedding drew closer, I had selected my best man, Dick Bocek. He was from the Martin Club *coterie* as was Vincent Joseph Michael Scully. Ray Kelly, my classmate at Iona, was also a groomsman and Dorothy's brother Guy, rounded out the group. Dorothy was attended by her cousin Sally as Matron of Honor and my cousin Judith as Maid of Honor. The ceremony and mass were, of course to be in her parish, Holy Family, and Fr. Leibfred was to officiate. The ceremony was scheduled for 10:30 a.m. on a Saturday. With the exception of Italian weddings, which were usually held on Sunday afternoons, Catholic weddings in the 1950s were normally held on Saturday mornings. After the wedding, the bridal party, who had been fasting prior to Communion since the previous midnight, went for a wedding breakfast. The, even then, unending series of photographs also took place during this period. Wedding guests, who mostly also needed breakfast, fended for themselves for an hour or two.

The reception, which in our case was held at the home of Dorothy's Aunt Irene, began an hour or two later. There were something in the vicinity of 75 guests and, to the best of my knowledge, a good time was had by all. My personal memories of the wedding and reception are few but acute. I remember her coming down the aisle on her father's arm and thinking how lovely she was. I remember refusing to pose for a "gag" photo of me falling backwards into the arms of my groomsmen and I remember sharing a piece of cake from a plate, on a fork. I confess to ignorance as to why newlyweds find it amusing to grind cake into one another's face (though more usually only the bride) having just promised to cherish each other. I remember posing for pictures with my father, Dorothy's family and the wedding party. All the Kane aunts and cousins were present. Since my father was, at the time, still embroiled in that feud with his family, only my Aunt Lilly from Saranac Lake represented the Kellys.

Somewhere in the day's proceedings, I remembered still another bit of advice from my mother:

Look not for beauty or softness of skin
But look for the heart that is loyal within
For beauty will fade and skin will grow old
But the heart that is loyal will never grow cold.

Somewhat unwittingly, I had followed her advice; with the bonus of a bonny bride.

We had only a brief honeymoon, four or five days, before classes started again. We went to the *Essex House Hotel*, off Central Park in Manhattan. We had a splendid time. In addition to connubial bliss, which at that time was often/usually deferred to the honeymoon, we tackled "the City" like children on holiday. We went to the Statue of Liberty, where I discovered that my lovely bride had a significant fear of heights. About one third of the way up the circular staircase, it so bothered her that we had to cross over and head back down. We also went for a ride on the Staten Island

Ferry. On the way back to Manhattan, just at dusk, a lightning storm dominated the skyline of the City in a truly dramatic and magnificent display. I had earlier mentioned that one our many shared affinities was affection for the great *Brooklyn Dodgers* teams of the 1950s. It turned out, Dorothy, who came from a family of *New York Giants* fans, was also a *Dodgers* fan. Early one afternoon, we grabbed a cab and went over the Brooklyn Bridge, from the *Essex House* to *Ebbets Field*, the old stadium which was the *Dodgers'* home park. There we saw the *Dodgers* play the *Giants.* Unbeknown to us, in early September of 1957, that was to be the last *Dodgers v. Giants* game played in *Ebbets Field.* Even today, in the quiet of a still summer night I will still sometimes indulge nostalgia and root for, or at least cheerfully remember, Hodges, and Peewee, Jackie and Carl, Campy and the Duke.

After our four or five days we returned to New Rochelle, to the flat (a third floor walkup), where my father and I had been living. He, quite graciously, had decided that since he and I would no longer be living together, he had no need for a two bedroom flat and would do me a favor by saving Dottie and me from having to search for a place to live. He would, as he pointed out, also save himself some rent money at the same time. It was a thoughtful gesture, and one we both appreciated.

And so that brief but lovely moment ended, and I returned to Iona for my junior year. I threw myself into my coursework, continued working and engaged in a modicum of extracurricular activity. A course load of twenty-one credits obviously absorbed the largest portion of my time. In the 1957-58 academic year I wrote about ten term papers of twelve to fifteen pages each, plus a number of shorter efforts. I also prepared for the usual number of quizzes, tests and recitations. In addition, there was the History Department's reading list. When a student declared as a History Major at Iona, he was provided with a copy of the departmental reading list, which featured 80 or so canonical books reflecting the current state of professional wisdom. The student then had two choices. He could select a number of books (I think it averaged about four per semester) to be read each term. He would then set about reading and taking notes. Then a meeting would be scheduled with his advisor to discuss each work. If he fulfilled this task to his advisor's satisfaction each term, he could be excused from taking a written departmental comprehensive examination during the spring term of his senior year. I particularly remember reading Ulrich B. Phillips' *Life and Labor in the Old South,* which I saw as rather an *apologia* for the American slave system and which I viewed quite negatively. I chose the path of reading, meeting and discussing. When I got to the spring of my senior year, with one less hurdle to be faced prior to graduation, I was pleased with my decision. I also discovered that the majority of my classmates had not made that choice. Copies of the notes that I (and others) had made prior to our meetings with our advisors, were at a premium prior to the exam. I was happy to make mine available to my friends – if *Xerox* machines had been readily available, the notes might have been more widely distributed. I think the system had real merit – though it did place a substantial burden on the faculty.

In those two years, I also became quite friendly with Dr. Chudoba and learned a great deal just walking about the campus and chatting about 20th Century politics, Church/State relations (he felt strongly that material prosperity posed the greatest moral danger to Catholicism), the history of the Slavic peoples and a variety of other topics ranging from the Hapsburgs to Czech composers such as Smetana and Dvorak. He was, or seemed to be, a man who stoically contained sadness. He was also one of the most interesting conversationalists I have ever met.

I also had a new job. I had been hired to work in the college library. There was slightly less money, but there was no commuting time. Then, very quickly, probably because I was a veteran, I was asked if I felt competent to run the library at night. That is, all the professional staff would go home, and an all student staff, under my direction, would run the library until closing. A modicum of extra money and a bit of authority – I was happy to accept. The college, of course, saved a bit of money, but, in fact, there were no decisions to be made at night, just the normal protocols to be followed. Everyone seemed satisfied.

I will confess to a minor element of corruption. I deliberately assigned myself the desk upstairs, with bound periodicals. Situated there, I was immediately available should I be needed. On the other hand, it was an area where regular student usage was minimal, so that I could, in fact, devote time to study with no loss to my normal or supervisory responsibilities. There I remained, ensconced for the most part until my graduation two years later. In the summer Brother Thomas, the Librarian, had me assist on various projects, some more interesting than others. On one occasion, the project involved a new Catholic High School, Bishop Gibbons, which was to be opened, by the Irish Christian Brothers, in Schenectady, NY. The new school needed the usual reference sources: dictionaries, atlases, encyclopedia, et al., which were specified on an approved list from the New York State Board of Regents. I spent several days roaming through the reference section of our library seeing what we had, whether we had duplicates and whether it or they matched the requirements. The resulting stack of books, reference and otherwise, was then bundled up and shipped to Schenectady. By a series of coincidences, I would follow the books a half dozen years later.

CHAPTER 7
Home: New Rochelle, Dorothy, Children – Grad School and Beyond

In the days after our wedding, Dorothy and I had a very unusual domestic establishment. We would awaken each morning and prepare for the day. She would leave for the train station (well within walking distance) and I would, weather and time permitting, either walk to Iona or grab a bus. She would return from the City around 6:00 p.m., walk home and wash the dishes and clean up after the previous night's supper and the day's breakfast. I would go to class, manage the evening session at the library, close up and come home. We would have dinner together at about 9:30 p.m. We would chat, smoke (we both smoked at the time, I about three packs a day), watch the late news and go to bed. Our weekends were much more traditional.

The euphoria of marriage came and then blended into a growth of admiration and affection. Life went on. Each of our families celebrated birthdays and anniversaries; a generation of cousins (our generation) was getting married, children were born and, on occasion there was a funeral and the sadness which followed. The tapestry of life was rewoven around us. Dorothy suffered a miscarriage, which wounded her deeply. Her obstetrician, Dr. Maffucci, proved a tower of strength, compassion and wisdom. It now seems archaic, even quaint, but he came to the house, climbed the three flights of stairs and took charge. He dealt with her physical needs and reassured her that the event was a natural one, containing no ominous portents for the future. Like most husbands in such circumstances, I was essentially useless; though listening to Maffucci was certainly a source of future wisdom for me. We resumed our normal course until, sometime in the late spring of 1958, Dot told me that she was, again, expecting a baby.

Our marriage, as well as my new part-time job, which eliminated commuting time, enabled me to significantly increase my academic productivity. I now had at least some study time available while I was working, which I really needed at the time because I was carrying a very heavy academic load (21 credits). As the fall term, 1958 started, Dorothy would be forced to give up her Eastman Kodak job once her pregnancy started to "show." That statement on paper now looks incredibly quaint, but was not an unusual requirement of the period. She was still "manfully" struggling with that antiquated typewriter and all the carbons then essential and, as she has always done, essentially propping me up in every way she could think of. The result was, for me, very pleasant. Fortunately for my future, as a prospective academic, the new circumstances were highly conducive to academic success. My junior and senior years would produce GPAs of 3.7 and 4.0. I could now present an academic record which graduate school admissions committees could consider without embarrassment. I was also fortunate enough, in my senior year, to be awarded a New York State Regents Teaching Scholarship. Based on academic record and a competitive exam (a sort of combined IQ and aptitude test), which provided, if memory serves, $2,500.00 a year for graduate study. Recipients were required to teach in New York State for a stipulated number of years. Since I never taught anywhere else, the requirement proved to be no impediment.

In the 1957-58 academic year I also experienced a political role reversal. I had previously sought to stage-manage college politics by persuading classmates to accept nominations for membership on the student council. Now, in spring 1958, I found "the biter bitten." A sort of *coup* in the veterans group took place, and I found myself the nominee. Rather more unsettling was the fact that I found myself elected. Fortunately, the term was the 1958-59 academic year when my academic load would be lighter. There were no startling developments, merely one more thing to be dealt with. The high point, if such there was, was when we led Iona's contingent up Fifth Avenue in the St. Patrick's Day Parade. After five years, as we marched past St. Patrick's Cathedral on 5th Ave., I finally had a relatively close look at my Korean "pal," Cardinal Spellman.

During the summer of 1958, I took two courses which allowed me to "catch up" with my class. I was no longer deficient in credits. All the work I missed in spring term 1956 had been completed. I was still working in the college library. We were trying to put aside a little money as Labor Day and the time when Dorothy would have to leave Eastman approached and we would lose her paycheck. In anticipation, and I suppose, youthful defiance (as well as joy at our first wedding anniversary), we took a Labor Day holiday to Washington, DC. There we saw the usual sights and went to a Washington *Senators* baseball game. The *Senators* were so bad that you could, and we did, just pop in and get box seat tickets ten minutes before the game. We enjoyed our time together, untrammeled by schedules or requirements. Thus, I entered my senior year. It would prove to be a busy, happy and productive year. By and large I very much enjoyed the courses I was taking and the professors who taught them. There were a few surprises. Professor Demetrius, who taught an elective course in Greek literature and culture, distributed the most impressive course bibliography I have ever seen. It included a suggested reading schedule. After about two weeks, I went to see him, because, while I was happy with the course, and enjoyed most of the readings, I could just not keep up. When I advised him of my problem, his response astonished me. "My boy," he said, "you are trying to read it all?" He then explained that the suggested reading list was, at best, a pious wish. He then offered a more manageable approach with a few emphasized readings. Operating on those principles, I continued to enjoy the course and, I think, took a good deal away from it. The year, also, virtually defined Liberal Arts, as I studied European and Asian history, as well as the history of Economic Ideas, an introductory psychology course and Special Ethics in philosophy. As a matter of coincidence I might note that many years later, that same phi-losophy teacher, Dr. Quick, would briefly join me on the faculty at Siena College. Among the few disappointments was a two semester course in speech, which I had taken as a potentially useful elective course for a po-tential teacher. I found it disappointingly banal.

Our domestic life was, quite literally, "enlivened" late in the first week of December (the Feast of St. Nicholas in fact) when Tom (Thomas O'-Connor Kelly III) was born. For what was a world altering event for us, it proved to be almost totally uneventful. December 6 fell on a Saturday in 1958. Dorothy and I were chatting after dinner when she told me she thought she was going into labor. After an interval to be sure, we called Dr. Maffucci and headed to New Rochelle Hospital. After the necessary forms were filled out and processed and Dot had been made as comfortable as the situation allowed, the good Doctor said, "she's fine, it's a first baby and, therefore, likely to take a while; why don't you go home and I will call you when the birth is likely." In those days, fathers were not welcome in or around delivery rooms, and New Rochelle Hospital did not even have an obstetric waiting room. Following his advice, I walked home, turned on the television and made myself a bourbon and water. As I sat down, the phone rang; it was Maffucci, and I was told to "get on back." Off I went. When I got there, Tommy had been born and Dottie was out like a light. When the Doctor began to lightly slap her face to awaken her, I told him to stop and let her rest. I would see her the following morning. I then walked home once again. When I sat down, I noticed that the ice in my highball had not yet had time to melt – but in that time, I had become a fa-ther! *Oh frabjous day! Callooh! Callay!* Dorothy, fortunately had had a relatively easy time, and, when I saw her the following morning, she was happy, content, and delighted with her son. After what was then the requi-site four or five day hospital stay, a cab delivered us back to the Franklin Ave. flat and the three of us began a new exploration of family.

As I looked forward to graduate school, I also realized that, because of the semester I had withdrawn from college; I would have a full year of GI

Bill money available for graduate school in 1959-1960. Because our only income after Dot left work was to be the GI Bill, maybe a part-time job and my scholarship, these considerations would be important to us. Since the per capita income in the U.S. for 1959, was $2,600.00, we were not facing destitution, but we were skating close to the limit. When it turned out that both the federal bureaucrats, re the GI Bill, and their state counter-parts, re the Regents Teaching fellowship, would prove unable to distribute the monies to which we were entitled for a period of several months that fall, we did approach penury until the first payments arrived. I still do not know how Dorothy, who was managing what money we had, managed to keep us afloat. Over the years, her skill in "robbing Peter to pay Paul" would prove almost arcane. On a few occasions, I thought I could do better. On each and every such occasion, I proved to be wrong.

We have, however, gotten ahead of our story. As I have indicated, the academic year of 1958-1959 proved to be a very successful one for us. The academic calendar, as it then existed, called for a Christmas holiday prior to final exams. After the New Year, there were about two weeks of classes, with finals scheduled from mid-January. Unlike the contemporary custom, where December is replete with pressure, anxiety and examinations, I had time to enjoy our son and begin to bond with him. Of course, as on so many occasions, I managed to find a way to get in trouble. A few days after mother and son returned to the Franklin Ave. flat, Dot asked me if he was not a beautiful baby. At that moment, he was still rather amorphous and his skin was peeling badly. I responded, without thinking, a besetting sin of mine, that he was "the scruffiest looking baby that I had ever seen." In my defense, he was not yet ready for a starring role. A mother's eye view, how-ever, encapsulates much more than that of a new father. I was not literally chastised, but Dorothy's response to my quip left me chagrined – and not for the first (nor the last) time.

My first such fall from grace had barely outlasted our honeymoon. On our first morning home (September 1957) Dot made a pot of coffee in our brand new Proctor Silex vacuum drip coffee pot. Neither of us had ever used one. She followed the directions punctiliously, and it produced the densest and most bitter cup of coffee I had ever consumed. As I tasted the coffee and put my cup down, she said: "You don't like it."

I had yet to learn any lessons about husbandly tact, and, since I was going up to the corner to get a morning paper, I just blurted out, "It's OK, I have to go out and get a paper anyway, I'll pick up a cup of coffee while I'm out." She drank a full cup to prove that it could be done, but it was abundantly clear that her new husband had been found to have feet of clay.

Fortunately, while I had term papers to write that Christmas (1959), most of the research was already done and there was time to convince my wife that I was not totally unfeeling and time to spend with the charming mite. I enjoyed the holidays completely. Unfortunately, I was a heavy sleeper and, after the first night home, I very rarely heard him cry out for a feeding during the night. Since Dorothy was, initially, breastfeeding, there was little I could have done in those early days. Later, when he was bottle-fed, I did, at least on rare occasions, prove to have some utility. It helped when we moved the crib into our bedroom, right at the foot of the bed. After several months, he slept through the night. On a very bright spring morning, I awoke and found Dot apprehensive – I think she was afraid that he had died during the night. Maybe she was just punchy from so much lost sleep. Anyway, she would not even look in the crib. After I looked and reassured her and she knew that he was hale and hearty and that *she would be getting more sleep,* her joy was palpable. We were a happy couple and delighted in our wonderful son.

As 1959 dawned, I realized that I was passing milestones. I had married, I was a father and I was about to become a college graduate. Between coursework, work at the library planning for graduate school and watching Tommy grow and his personality develop, the Spring of 1959 passed rapidly. I did march in the Saint Patrick's Day parade that March, and Dorothy and I joined several parties later in the day. I have still never discovered the why or wherefore of green beer, but the events were pleasant enough. After that glimpse of Cardinal Spellman, it would only be two and a half months later that I would see him again as he presided over my graduation. He was the prototype of the perfect graduation speaker. Since he presided over all Catholic College graduations in the Archdiocese, he harbored no false hopes that anyone cared what he said. The result was that he spoke for well under five minutes, announced a generous gift to the college and sat down. Regrettably, there always seems to be one graduation speaker who assumes that someone actually cares about what he or she is saying and releases a torrent of words. In any event, like all such rituals, the rites ended and the celebrations began. Tommy, then just about six months old, was present, albeit rather indifferent, in his mother's arms. I don't think there was any way I could have been happier.

After Tom's birth, we considered our future. After much thought and some discussion, we once again primarily relied on optimism. Relying on faith in the future and hope, we moved forward with the plans we had made. Given that there were now three of us, we knew that we could not afford to spread a wide geographic net in our search for graduate schools. Since we were in metropolitan New York with its plethora of colleges and universities, that had never seemed very important in any event. I think we came to focus on Fordham University quite early. It was affordable, it was nearby (in the Bronx, with reasonable access by bus) and of good reputation. And so, application forms were acquired, filled out and filed with the office of graduate admissions. I never even applied for a scholarship or fellowship. (I thought that awful/wonderful 1956-57 academic year of overloads and courtship, et al., seemed a very heavy burden.) Not quite as confidently as in 1955, I once again put a lot of eggs in a single basket, and, once again, the basket was not dropped. I was admitted to the doctoral program in history for the fall term, 1959. Our economic assumptions were that by using my remaining year of eligibility from the GI Bill, plus my New York State Regents Teaching Fellowship monies, I would be able to complete the two semesters of fulltime residence necessary for the doctoral program. After that, depending on circumstances I would continue in residence or, if unable, seek a teaching job and move to part-time graduate study. In what now seems a ridiculous oversight, I did not seek either fellowships or scholarships for 1960-1961.

In the fall of 1959, we skated on the brink of economic disaster as those bureaucratic blunders at the Veterans Administration and the New York State Department of Education multiplied and, for the first three months of the term, we received no money from either source. In addition, our checking account was in the same bank as my father's and the bank consistently debited our account for my father's checks. Not once did they ever debit his account for ours. After several months we solved the problem by switching banks, but it had greatly added to our financial anxiety and the consequent turmoil. Only Dorothy's skills at both household budgeting and money management kept us afloat. As we talked of bills versus available funds, I lived with fears of some modern equivalent of debtor's prison. My wife somehow managed to at least give the appearance of serenity.

When September came, I took the bus ride to the Bronx each day and began my graduate study at Fordham. I was gratified to find that my lifelong desire to become an historian was being validated by my graduate school experience. My program was in American History, with a minor in English Constitutional History from the Middle Ages to the end of the Stuart Monarchs. All entering graduate students were required to take an introductory course in the philosophy of history and historiography. The professor, a Jesuit priest known colloquially as "Jolly Cholly," was quick to declare himself. "How do you tell the difference between an Oxford man and a Cambridge man?" As dutiful graduate students, we all declared our ignorance. "An Oxford man walks down the street like he owns it. A Cambridge man walks down the street like he doesn't give a damn who owns it." "Cholly" was a Cambridge man. He also created a stir by suggesting that he had voted for the election of Eisenhower. Even in those days, most academics were rather more liberal than the common ruck, and the press had crowned Stevenson as an intellectual, an "egghead." Addressing the stir in the class that this had caused, he went on: "Stevenson for cocktails;

Eisenhower for president." Few of my professors at Fordham were as amusing or as colorful but all were highly competent.

There were some "stars" on the graduate faculty at Fordham. Robert Remini was then emerging as one of the premier scholars of the "Age of Jackson." Fr. Vincent Hopkins, SJ whose book, *Dred Scott's Case* was largely considered definitive at that time, was also ascending and, among the older group, there was Oskar Halecki, another World War II exile whose command of Polish and Central European History was magisterial. Halecki, then nearly seventy, was a delight as a lecturer, likely to make a point, look up and, quite unselfconsciously, say something like, "I remember, when I was working in the archives in Vienna in 1915 and ...." I very much enjoyed his class, as I did my time with Father Hopkins. There was a rather eclectic and totally unorganized group of students (to which I was drawn), who deliberately avoided Remini because his idea of a research paper was to hand a student a roll of microfilm from a significant figure of the age of Jackson to transcribe. Somehow he managed a system to assign grades to the transcriptions. I am sure the results were productive for his scholarship and perhaps for his students, but it seemed egregiously unfair and boring to boot. Those faculty members who might not have been defined as stars seemed to me to be both talented lecturers and meticulous mentors.

At that time Fordham offered two approaches to the Master's Degree. One was to take twenty-four credits (eight courses) and then write a thesis (six credits). The other was the completion of thirty credits (ten courses). Both required passing a language competency exam and a comprehensive examination, which, in my case, involved both American and European history. I decided that the second alternative made more sense for me. I would, probably in a year and a summer, complete the coursework, satisfy the residency requirement for the doctoral program and, should it be necessary, have an option to seek employment. With the exception of the summer school plans, it pretty much worked out that way

Our domestic economy did receive a substantial boost at Christmas time of that year.as I was fortunate enough to snag a seasonal job with the

U.S. Post Office. Christmas hires were highly desirable among impecunious academics because they paid very well (compared with most part-time jobs) and fit beautifully into the gaps in the academic calendar. No schedule juggling was necessary. I was assigned to a branch in the Bronx. It was a rewarding position in several senses of the word – first, monetarily. It was the best hourly salary I ever received. Secondly, it was particularly interesting in that it offered an insight into the bureaucratic mind. My group of seasonal employees were hired as clerks; we were to sort mail in preparation for delivery. We reported to work at midnight and sorted mail into the proper boxes for the mailmen (the then approved usage) to deliver the next morning. Our shift was scheduled to end at 7:00 a.m.

Suddenly, about 5:30 a.m., we were all summoned to the front of the building and told to grab a mailbag, as we were going to be assigned routes to deliver. We protested; it was not what we had been hired for, and we did not know the area which would significantly complicate the process. The manager, who seemed to be at least a three star bureaucrat, told us that if we wished to be paid for as full shift, delivery was a non-negotiable fact. We came to realize that it was a *fait accompli,* we had to deliver mail. We also began to understand that it also meant we would be getting overtime. We yielded. As we left the building with our mailbags, we realized that at 5:30 a.m. on a December morning, the sun had not risen in the Bronx. A fulltime postal employee then led us up the block to a coffee shop where the floor was already almost completely covered with full mail bags. We added ours. At government expense (salary), we all had bacon and eggs, juice, and drank coffee while we waited for the sun to come up. Then we delivered the mail. How much the bureaucratic *fait accompli* cost the government, I do not know – but there were an awful lot of mailbags on the floor of that shop for the best part of two hours that morning, and all the rest of the mornings until Christmas.

Dottie and I continued to learn about each other, to blend our tastes and lifestyles and to enjoy Tommy's growth. There is a real joy in watching a baby, largely amorphous at birth, begin to grow and to watch a personality begin to emerge. Shortly after I graduated from Iona, we also became aware that Dorothy was pregnant again. Our second child would be due just about the end of the second term of my graduate work at Fordham, in the spring of 1960. Clearly, with my eligibility for funds from the GI Bill exhausted, there would be no way in which I could afford to continue full-time graduate study. I still have no idea why I did not explore the possibility of scholarships or fellowships at Fordham, other than it just did not occur to me. Faced with real imperatives, I turned my attention to finding work.

Since it was still my intention to become a college professor, a teaching position seemed to be the next logical step. Since I had never taken any education courses at either Iona or Fordham, I knew a New York State Teaching certificate was a near impossibility. I, therefore, turned my attention to the Roman Catholic High Schools in the vicinity. At that time few, if any, Catholic schools required a teaching certificate. Many, probably an overwhelming majority, now do. I cannot speak to the gains attributed to the credential. I interviewed at one New York City public school and perhaps four or five Catholic schools. The public school was a disheartening experience. It was so out of control that the principal was willing to waive the certification requirement in order to provide enough bodies to staff the building. An on-site interview clearly demonstrated that teaching in that environment, while well remunerated, would be more custodial than academic. While sympathetic to its problems, I was unable to give it serious consideration. Of the Catholic schools, the most interesting was certainly Regis High School. It was, and is, a highly selective Jesuit-run high school, which is invariably very highly rated on virtually all lists of "best of...," "most highly rated ...," etc. All students were on full scholarship. I have always regretted that the salary being offered was so low that given the cost of commuting into the City, subway fare, etc., I was unable to even consider accepting an opportunity to teach there. As it turned out, on balance, the best offer I had available was from Archbishop Stepinac High School in White Plains, New York. After an extensive but very pleasant interview there, Monsignor Nolan, the principal, offered me $4,200.00 a year, with a daily teaching load of five courses. Class size normally ran from 35 to 40 students, and I usually taught somewhere around 190 students. I think such a load currently would be considered a violation of the XIIIth Amendment to the Constitution, i.e., the reintroduction of slavery. The pay was low but, like the size of the classes, by the standards of 1960, was not unconscionable. Access to the school was also made easier by the fact that I had turned twenty-five that August. When I left the Army, at twenty, I could have afforded to purchase a car, or to insure a car, but not both. At twenty-five, insurance rates became reasonable, and Dot and I had embarked on a search. As it happened, it only took us across the street.

With a second child expected, we decided we needed a bit more space and so we left the Franklin Ave. flat and relocated to White Oak St. and another third floor walkup. With some irony, the new place found us almost directly across the street from the main entrance to Iona, behind the College Diner, which had often been a favorite spot for the Faithful Seventeen to gather before or after a function. It was also much closer to the Schillers, well within walking distance. On the other side of the street was a small house inhabited by two quite elderly ladies, who drove a 1948 Plymouth Club Coupe. As luck would have it, just as we realized that we now needed a car (though we had little money with which to buy it) the woman who drove, died. The survivor did not drive and so the car became available. An ensuing visit resulted in our acquiring a dark green, standard shift, six cylinder, 1948 Plymouth. In return, we handed over $65.00. Though that now sounds like scamming an elderly woman, it was pretty much the standard price for a car of that age and that condition at the time. At first, it burned an inordinate amount of oil, almost a quart per week. However, petroleum products were quite inexpensive at the time (gasoline was about thirty-one cents per gallon) and so we ignored it. (I did, once or twice, think of Lt. Jones and my adventures with a deuce and a half.) As time went on and the car was driven regularly, both gasoline and oil consumption improved. I assume we just burned a lot of gunk out. In any event, it gave us good service for most of the next few years.

Our second son, Terry (Terrence Kane Kelly) had entered the world in mid-May, 1960. The timing was a trifle awkward, but, as the world knows, when a child decides to be born, it gets born! I was in the middle of spring term final exams when we headed to New Rochelle Hospital once again. Young Master Thomas was, rather unceremoniously, delivered to his grandparents. Once again, it was evening, but this time the scenario was different. I was not dismissed, but banished to the hospital lobby. (There was still no obstetrical waiting room.) There I spent the night.

I was scheduled to take a final examination in Anglo-American Foreign Policy at 4:30 that afternoon. I had been alert enough to bring texts and notes with me and, as I waited, seemingly interminably, for the birth, I was not at a loss for something to do. About 2:30 or 3:00 a.m., a "swamper," who was mopping the lobby floor, took pity on me and brought me a cup of coffee. It must have been on a warmer half the night. It was foully bitter and may have been the worst cup of coffee I have ever tasted, and I was really grateful for it. It gave me a moment of human contact and a caffeine boost I really needed. Sometime between five and six in the morning, I was informed that Terry had been born. Other than the time factor, the birth had been uneventful and Dottie did not seem stressed. After seeing them both, I went home and fell into bed. Before I headed to Fordham and my final, I got back to the hospital and saw the baby again and briefly chatted with Dorothy. (At this distance in time, it seems both silly and arrogant, but at the time I was quite pleased with myself when I found out that I had "aced" the exam. Now, I can only think that I probably never, before or since, had quite so much time to devote to undisturbed study for a single test.)

That summer found me actually earning real money. A family we knew casually, the husband taught English literature at a nearby women's college, ran a summer day camp. He was the director and, in effect, head counselor, preparing schedules, supervising games and so on. He was on the cusp of finishing his doctorate and needed a bloc of time to complete his dissertation. The solution they projected was for him to take the summer off and work on the dissertation. In his absence, I would replace him. It would be a "win, win" – he would finish his degree and I, after a near starvation year at Fordham, would actually have a livable income. I would begin each day driving a Volkswagen van. I would pick up eight or ten campers (the counselors would each do the same) and bring them to the camp. During the course of the day, I made sure that the schedule was maintained, supervised the counselors, and then delivered the campers back to their homes. His wife continued to perform the duties she controlled: organizational, crafts, etc., and correct me if I wandered too far from normal protocols. It was far and away the best summer offer I had ever had. When it ended, our fiscal position was as good as it had ever been since the day we married. Additionally, I was probably in the best physical condition I had been in since basic training: sound in wind and limb (though still smoking three packs a day) and even, despite my very light-skinned Irish tendency to burn and peel, rather well tanned.

As summer ended, still practicing my new driving skills, I turned my attention to Stepinac High School. I had accepted the offer made by Monsignor Nolan (see above), and I was excited about my first teaching job. The school was directed under the auspices of the Archdiocese of New York and was of reasonable size, about 1300 boys. There were, at that time about 60 instructors and administrators, all male, only two of whom were laymen. The overwhelming majority of the faculty were priests and religious brothers.

My interview and agreement with Monsignor Nolan had taken place in May, and, thereafter, I had heard nothing. In July, I called the school and made arrangements to go up to White Plains and pick up a copy of the textbook the department had chosen for World History. When the first day of school came around, I presented myself at the school office, introduced myself and asked to be directed to my classrooms. There was a bit of confusion before one of the older women staffing the office came over to me , indicated that I was expected and said, "There has been a change in your schedule and you are teaching a section of ninth grade civics. Would you like a copy of the text?" While I loathe bureaucracy and abominate paperwork, this exceptionally casual system and attitude flabbergasted me. If I had lost a World History section and gained a Civics section, that was hardly the end of the world. That as a new and totally inexperienced teacher I would have to face even one section totally unprepared, even for a day, was a serious matter. I indicated that, yes I really would like to have a copy of the text and, remembering my mother's not infrequent usage of the old English maxim "In for a penny, in for a pound," I went in search of my classrooms.

Stepinac and its faculty in September of 1960 represented the triumphalist period of the Catholic Church in the United States. Of between 50 and 60 faculty members and administrators (exempting gym teachers and coaches), there were only two of us who were laymen. Before I left, two and a half years later, that number would quadruple and then continue to climb with the later decline of religious vocations. The faculty was an unusual mix. As a member of the parochial school system created and maintained by the Archdiocese of New York, it was administered and partially staffed by secular priests of the archdiocese. There were also priests and brothers of the Crosiers, an order following the rule of St. Augustine, which dates to the early 13th century, and priests and brothers of the Oblates of St. Francis de Sales one of whose principal missions is education. There were also brothers of the Xaverian order assigned to the school. The students were primarily from Westchester County and varied widely in academic proficiency, as might be assumed if one realizes that, ranked on a descending scale, sophomore year classes ranged from 2A to 2K. The faculty considered the range so great that, jokingly, based on the idea that Catholic schools were overly selective, we spoke of Stepinac as a "baptized public school." It was, for me, a difficult, challenging and overall wonderful experience. I probably never learned as much in such a short period of time as I did at Stepinac.

In that sense, I wish, for the sake of those who were my first students, that I could have a "do over" on that first year of teaching. I was too wedded to the textbook and the New York State syllabus, which prevented me from providing a richer and more complex view of the subject matter. I learned from that, but I still regret my rigidity. I was also overly idealistic. I thought that my students and I would somehow embark on an educational adventure. My students, much more realistic, realized that they had an opportunity for control. Their adventure would be to play Long John Silver to my Jim Hawkins in this version of *Treasure Island.* Having begun the term seeking to be a comrade or a companion, like many naive teachers before me, I found that to establish sufficient *gravitas* to actually teach them, I would need to convert from comrade to commissar. This would enable me to at least teach, but only at substantial emotional cost. It was another area for regret. One sign of the nervous energy required by this amended conduct was that my physician prescribed mild tranquilizers for me well before Thanksgiving. Slowly I fought my way back to at least a semblance of control. By January, I was probably somewhere near average as an instructor while still highly dissatisfied with my performance.

In the meantime, I was navigating my cultural introduction to teaching in a Catholic high school. Overall, since much mirrored my own high school experience, I was comfortable from the beginning. Since my primary assignment was teaching World History, I was teaching sophomores along with one section of freshmen. Almost from the beginning, I found myself at school on Saturday mornings. That was when the junior varsity football team played its games, and most JV players were sophomores. I was probably teaching half of the team. The kids were happy to see me, and I was gaining some credibility with them as a potential mentor. Over my two and a half years at Stepinac, one JV team or another would remain a constant for me since so many of my students were on the teams. I would later teach some American History (the junior class) as well.

I also was learning that in the day to day working of an institution, flow charts do not necessarily reflect reality. At Stepinac, on everyday matters as opposed to policy, the "go to" guy was not a named administrator, but Ray Morris, the attendance clerk. He operated out of a small office, almost an enlarged closet, just inside the main door to the school. If you needed something, or needed to have something done, you could follow established procedures and, sooner or later, the issue would be handled. On the other hand, if you called Ray he would usually see to it that the issue would be resolved, if not that day, certainly overnight. He was a very pleasant man and a very useful ally.

Outside school hours, there was normally very little contact between clerical and lay faculty. That was not surprising; we were an inconsequential percentage of the faculty, about 2% or less and not available for chats at communal dinner or breakfast, as was the rest of the faculty. There was one notable exception. Early in the fall term, there was a faculty reception and dinner, a welcome, as it were, to which all were invited. (In the first year, I was the only lay faculty member in attendance.) Dorothy was concerned that clerical asceticism would provide a dining experience inadequate to my needs – unsure, as it were, that I could get by on a diet of lentils and leeks. As it turned out, it was rather more a Lucullan feast. On arrival, one was greeted with an abundance of pre-prandial drinks. The school's chief financial officer was presiding over a punch bowl full of Manhattan cocktails. To prove that no discrimination was intended, there were Martinis as well. There was a happy hubbub of conversation during which I found myself chatting with one of the brothers who had spent a good deal of time in Africa. He loved the school but really wanted to get back to Africa where he could "wear his whites." The occasion was purely sociable and markedly convivial. I had not had any qualms about getting on with my peers, but if I had, that occasion would have set them at rest. It was later than I had anticipated (probably around 10:00 or 10:30 p.m. when I got home. Dot was waiting, prepared to feed me should it be necessary). Her first question was, "what did you have to eat?" Her expression and her interest changed markedly when I replied, "*Coq au vin.*"

On a substantially less collegial note, on the second or third day of the term, the vice-principal entered my class with a student in tow. He informed me that he was assigning the student to my class. I told the student to try and find a seat and told the vice-principal that I would like a moment of his time, in the hall. I brought my roll book with me and showed it to him.

Those roll books had forty lines for student names. I said, "Father, I have filled every line on this roll book page, I have even used the margin line to make a forty-first line but, I will be damned if I will start another page." Other arrangements were then made. The vice-principal, Father Sullivan, was a vital part of the administration and, in particular, of the disciplinary structure of the school. That, of course, made him, from the student point of view, the designated villain. He also had a slight tendency to corpulence and, like me, had a crew cut. In the two or three years prior to 1960, the film *The Bridge on the River Kwai* had enjoyed immense popularity. The great Japanese actor Sessue Hayakawa had played the cruel prisoner-of-war camp commandant in that film. Hayakawa also wore a crew cut and had a tendency to corpulence. The students, conflating his administrative role and a few small physical characteristics with adolescent cruelty, but, I am convinced, with absolutely no racial overtones, universally called Fr. Sullivan, "The Jap."

It was, and is, of course, a part of adolescent humor to delight in finding ways to amuse themselves at the expense of authority. On one occasion their opportunity began at lunch time. There was a small faculty and staff lunchroom, behind the student cafeteria. It was used mostly by staff since the religious faculty had their own dining facilities upstairs. I often ate there as well. A small group of us, including the school nurse (a woman named Alice) was at lunch and, as people left, the group dwindled down to Alice and me. As we got up to leave, we realized that somehow, the door leading back into the cafeteria had been locked. There was an alternate route and, I as began to tell Alice about it, she began to beat on the cafeteria door and demand that it be opened. Knowing what was likely to happen, I vainly tried to get her to stop. Before that happened, a couple of the boys opened the door. When it opened, three or four hundred boys were intensely focused on it and as the two of us walked out, the wolf howls and whistles came close to raising the roof! The only course available was to walk away, cherishing whatever shreds of dignity could be found.

As I hope I have made clear, discipline was a major problem for me in 1960-1961. In theory, Stepinac did not allow faculty to strike pupils. However, just as when I was a student at Timon, priests and brothers, who felt the necessity, were not prepared "to spare the rod." Indeed, I remember one of my favorite colleagues, upon being asked by a parent at Parent's Night, how he motivated his students, replied, "Some I pat on the back, others a little lower." When I started teaching, I had told myself that if I ever struck a student, I would somehow have lost the battle. That is, I would have failed my ideal. After about a two months of teaching 180-190 fifteen and six-teen-year-old sophomore boys, at their most obstreperous, I found myself saying, "OK, you've lost." Once they were aware that I was willing to play the game, the furor and the shouting slowly died. In future years, I adopted a different persona. Each September, I turned to the *modus operandi* of older teachers. I drew on the old adage, "Don't smile until Christmas, and don't laugh until Easter." My first class began with an extensive view of how much work needed to be done for the entire year and what I would re-quire from each student. I also made sure to assign a reasonably heavy homework assignment for the first night. The new *persona* seemed to work much better than the idealist of September, 1960. There were markedly fewer classroom disruptions and much more work was accomplished. I think it true also to note that the experience of 1960-1961 made me a more effective teacher. In any event the year made life simpler for me and cer-tainly more productive for my students.

1960 was, of course, also a presidential election year. The candidates were Richard M. Nixon, the incumbent Republican vice president and John F. Kennedy, the Democratic candidate who was the junior Senator from Massachusetts. Kennedy was a Roman Catholic, which brought a piquant flavor to the election. (It also meshed well with Catholic triumphalism.) Many could remember the furor raised in 1928 by the candidacy of the only other Roman Catholic candidate, Al Smith. My father had never, in my memory, which went back to 1940, voted for a candidate of the Dem-ocratic Party. He was a Kennedy stalwart in 1960. It annoyed him no end if anyone suggested that his affection for Kennedy was merely due to his Irish Catholicism. I raised the point, tongue in cheek, with some frequency.

Personally, I stood in support of Nixon. He was the heir to the policies of Eisenhower and, based on their records in the House and Senate, Nixon seemed the more serious candidate.

I actively campaigned, attended rallies, recruited college students from Iona and the College of New Rochelle (CNR) and made myself generally useful to the local campaign. In my classes, I tried to stand neutral. If a student asked a question, I tried to answer objectively. So, I might say that the Nixon or Kennedy campaign stood for principle A because they thought it achieved goal X. On the other hand the opponent opposed goal A because they felt it was more likely to produce result Z. As the end of the campaign approached, I think on Monday before the election, I devised a crude measure to gauge how successful my quest for objectivity had been. I asked each student to take a blank sheet of paper and indicate above the fold, which candidate he preferred and then, below the fold, which candidate he thought I was voting for. I was very pleased with the results. I had a slightly better than 85% correlation. If the student favored Nixon, he was quite sure I had voted for Kennedy and *vice versa*.

I also found myself, somewhat belatedly, returning to the campus of CNR, recruiting young women to work for Nixon. Election returns ran much later than the current curfew (there were still such things) for CNR students, so that quite late on election night/morning, I found myself engaged in sneaking the girls back on campus well after curfew. The titillating aspects of that scenario were obviated because Dorothy was actively assisting.

Sophomores were my stock in trade from 1960-1963 as I continued to primarily teach World History. I found them, overall, even in that first year, exhilarating. They were inquisitive and they were fearless. By junior year, the students had already begun to become cautious. They were worried about their "permanent record" and its impact on college admissions and with that worry questions became less adventurous. Sophomores were still adventurers. Their questions might only be dubiously related to the material immediately under discussion, but almost all of them could be tweaked in a way to develop or clarify a point. On one occasion, though, a pre-planned student question arose, not to advance the lesson, but to embarrass the instructor. For some reason, which I never understood, we had one very odd period each day. I taught the class for twenty-two minutes and then they broke and went to lunch. After lunch they returned for the second half of the class. They always returned refueled and very antsy. One day, when I had been focused on teaching **world geography**, they went to lunch. When we returned, and I opened the door to the classroom, I noticed that every student was in his seat; there was absolute quiet and all were looking straight ahead – "butter would not have melted in their mouths." Like any other teacher I knew that there was to be a challenge of some sort – they were very happy. As was my custom with that particular class, after lunch I always began by asking if there were any questions. I don't know who asked the question; it may have been Bob Hyland who later played center for Green Bay and New York (I do remember that he and a number of other football players were in that class). The question was, "Mr. Kelly, I don't remember; where are the Islands of Langerhans?" The class was absolutely still and so for about two seconds was I. Then, suddenly, I was back in 10th grade at Timon in Father Ambrose Buckingham's biology class. With just a touch of humor in my voice, and no intimation as to how close to success they had been, I responded, "In your pancreas." And that is how reputations for something approaching academic omniscience are born.

In August of 1961, Dorothy and I were overjoyed to welcome our first daughter, our third child. She was baptized Dorothy Marie Kelly, which we thought a lovely name. Always her own woman, she early disliked her name and became, and remains, Dorrie. I think we both thought of daughters as doll-like creatures, to be cuddled and cosseted and petted. Once again, our daughter marched to the beat of a different drummer. She, from her earliest days, evinced a *nolo me tangere* quality. She rarely consented to being held or cuddled. She would, if frightened or hurt, accept consolation until she was satisfied that she understood or controlled the situation or circumstances. After that, her independence was quickly reasserted. She was obviously a bright and curious child and her birth was an adornment to what had been a very interesting year for our family. A year of growth, of adaptation, of maturation and of joy.

My second year at Stepinac saw the number of lay faculty expand to about six. Clearly, changes were coming in Catholic education. A few administrators and members of the clerical faculty began to refer to me, only partly in jest, as the "dean of the lay faculty," in view of my seniority. I had been there **two whole years!** I felt thoroughly at home. I now had a reputation, and students were much less likely to try me on, which made teaching easier, more joyful and more productive. As I began to look forward to the 1962-63 academic year, Dot and I sat down for a serious discussion as to what we might do with the rest of our working lives. The upshot of the conversation was that at Stepinac I was becoming a large fish in a very small pond. The school was an excellent fit for me, and I was learning and growing. On the other hand, if I was to realize my ambition of becoming a college teacher, time was fleeting. There was no time like the present; if I was to take a chance, now was the time. As always, Dorothy had more confidence in me than I did and it was decided that we would test the waters. *Carpe diem!* What opportunities might be found? Unsure as to how to proceed, I placed my name, references and credentials with a professional placement service and sat back to wait. By that time I had completed my MA and had an additional six credits toward the doctorate. In today's circumstances, a college placement would be almost inconceivable. In 1962, in many undergraduate institutions a quite large percentage of the faculty taught with no degree beyond the MA, a few even with only the BA.

After a relatively short wait, in the early Fall, I was informed that an appropriate vacancy existed at Siena College, located upstate, in Loudonville, NY, just outside Albany. As with most of my recent past, the college was operated under Roman Catholic auspices, specifically by the Franciscans – the Order of Friars Minor: who had taught me at Timon. Siena, like Iona and Timon before it, was an all-male institution, though women were admitted into the evening division. I responded and an appointment was made at the college for the requisite interviews. As it happened, my mother's sister, my Aunt Anne, was at that time living in Albany and suggested that I stay with her while in the area. Aside from familial affection, economics also played a role in my grateful acceptance. On the appointed day, I arrived for the interview and learned that the vacancy resulted from the untimely death of a highly respected professor named Frank Monaghan. The order of the interviews seemed odd. I had more or less assumed that I would start with the department, move through the Liberal Arts Division and so on until the end of the process. Instead, I was greeted by Father Matthew Conlin, Head of the Arts Division. After my interview with Fr. Matthew, he took me to the office of the President, Father Edmund Christie. That was more a cheerful chat than a formal interview. I then met with the Dean of the College [now the Academic Vice-President], who turned out to be Father Brian Duffy, my former English teacher and Dean of Discipline at Timon. That interview was the most penetrating. After discussing my credentials, my academic record and my teaching experience, we wandered a bit and ended up with some discussion of the "old days" at Timon. He then delivered me to the Department head, Father Michael McCloskey, for a rather cursory interview. When I returned to my Aunt Anne's after the interviews, she asked me how I thought it had gone. I replied that I thought rather well and concluded, "When the Dean turned me over to the department head and left, his last words to Fr. Michael were, 'Take good care of him; he's one of my former students.'"

During the interviewing process, there was one point that concerned both sides. Siena wanted to know if I was under contract and, if so, what terms applied to departure. I was not, nor ever had been, under contract – always just a handshake. I was, however, concerned that Stepinac should have an appropriate amount of time to replace me. I indicated that I thought two months would be a necessary minimum and said that if that could not be met, I did not think, in good conscience, I could accept an offer. (Stepinac was fully aware of my activities during the period, and a number of my references were from administrators and colleagues.) I had also felt some trepidation about salary. In my third year at Stepinac, I was now making around $5200.00 a year and feared some loss of income. Since the salary for the post was $5700.00 a year, that fear vanished.

About two and a half weeks after the interview, I got a letter from Siena. It contained an offer and a contract for Jan. 1, 1963 to Dec. 31, 1963. I kissed my wife, hugged the children, signed the contract and mailed it back. I went into see Monsignor Nolan the next morning and told him I would be leaving in mid-January and thanked him for his confidence in hiring me in 1960. A number of my clerical colleagues surprised me before I left with an informal but warm and convivial party, during which a number of flattering things were said, which I still remember with great joy. Few, I think, ever received a semiofficial proclamation as "Favorite Former Faculty Member." My students too, in various ways, including stopping by the apartment, flattered me by their reaction to my leaving.

In a way, I had come full circle. Born in the Northern part of the state (Port Henry) I had been raised in central and Western New York (Syracuse and Buffalo). I had, in the course of growing up, come to the Metropolitan Area (New Rochelle) where I enlisted in the army. I had then gone to college and graduate school, begun my professional career, married and started a family, all as at least a quasi "imperial" New Yorker. Now, I was about to begin the fulfillment of a lifelong goal. I had an appointment as a college instructor. I was heading into a very familiar environment (academic, male, small, Catholic) and I was heading home. We were going Upstate!

APPENDIX A
Morse Code

Alphabet	Numbers	Cut Numbers
A = .-	1 = .————	1 = .-
B = _...	2 = ..———	2 = ..-
C = -..	3 ...——	3 = .—
E = .	4 = ...-	4 = ...-
F = ..-.	5 = ...	5 = ...
G = —.	6 = -....	6 = -...
H = ...	7 = —...	7 = —.
I = ..	8 = —..	8 = -..
J = ——.	9 = ————.	9 = -.
K = -.-	0 = —————	0 = -
L = ..-.		
M = —	**Procedural Signals**	
N = -.	CQ – Calling any station	
O = ——	AR – Over to you	
P = .——.	K – Go ahead (transmit)	
Q = ——.-	R – Received	
R = .-.	CL – Clear Finished (clear/going off air)	
S = ...		
T = -		
U = ..-		
V = ...-		
W = .——		
X = -..-		
Y = -.——		
Z = —..		

Appendix B

Ranks, U.S. Army – 1952
Commissioned and Enlisted

Enlisted – Rank and Insignia

E-1 – Essentially an untrained recruit – lowest rank, no insignia

E-2 – Automatic step in pay grade after basic training, no insignia

E-3 – Private First Class (PFC) – 1 stripe (chevron)

E-4 – Corporal – first non-commissioned officer grade, two stripes

E-5 – Staff sergeant – three stripes and a lower arc of one bar uniting them

E-6 – Sergeant first class – three stripes and an arc of two bars

E-7 – Master Sergeant – three stripes and an arc of three bars

Commissioned Officers – Rank and Insignia

O-1 - 2nd Lieutenant – one rectangular gold bar

O-2 - 1st Lieutenant – one rectangular silver bar

O-3 - Captain – two rectangular silver bars

O-4 - Major – one gold oak leaf

O-5 - Lieutenant Colonel – one silver oak leaf

O-6 - Colonel – one silver eagle

O-7 - Brigadier General – one silver star

O-8 - Major General – two silver stars

O-9 - Lieutenant General – three silver stars

O-10 - General – four silver stars

O-11 - General of the Army – five silver stars. Currently vacant – no officer who did not exercise command in World War II has ever held this rank.

NB: In the Army, "Silver ranks gold" – thus the silver bar of a 1st Lieutenant outranks the gold bar of a second Lieutenant and the silver oak leaf of a Lieutenant Colonel outranks the gold leaf of a major.

There exists an additional cohort, between officers and enlisted men – Warrant Officers. There are many more warrants now than there were in the early 1950s. It seemed to add needless complexity to the narrative to include them and so, with apologies, I have not.

ACKNOWLEDGMENTS

I have always felt that my life has been blessed in many ways. Not the least of which has been the number and variety of the people who have played both in the life and in the crafting of the book.

The inception of the book certainly owes less to me than to my children, particularly Terry and Dorrie who, each in his or her own way, indicated that it should be undertaken and sooner rather than later. Tom and Eileen and Maureen and Kathleen offered reasonably enthusiastic seconds to the motion. *Sorry it took so long.*

As the dedication is intended to indicate, little of worth has taken place in my life, since Jan. 27, 1956, without the warmth and strength of the support provided by my wife Dorothy. Her sagacity and serenity have been a rock for me personally as well as professionally.

Over the years, friends and colleagues have been generous in offering their support for volumes I have written or edited. The staff of the Siena College Library, particularly John Vallely, Sean Maloney and Bill Kanalley have always been unstinting with their time and virtually endless with their patience. I am grateful for many years of friendship as well as professional service. So too, over my career, faculty colleagues both within and outside the department have done much to refresh ideas, prevent errors and offer critical thought. I think particularly of Bob Hoeffner, Jim Harrison, Bruce Eeelman, Len Cutler and Paul Dwyer (both a colleague and a former student) who have brought so much to my life and were always prompt to respond to any request for aid.

Particular attention should be drawn to three colleagues who have borne more than their fair share of the heat of the day.

Doug Hoyt is a Siena alumnus, and a former member of Siena's English department faculty who is now retired from the New York State Education Dept. He has labored mightily in this particular vineyard. No one has read more drafts of this mss. than Doug. His comments, always offered with great gentleness and civility (with all severity tactfully dispensed) were invaluable. I cannot offer sufficient thanks.

Doug Lonnstrom of Siena's Finance and Business Mathematics Dept., who has been my long-time partner since the foundation of the Siena Research Institute, has also been a perceptive and sensitive reader whose suggestions have often proved wise and pointed. Doug also enlisted his wife, another a good friend. Cris' readings always seemed to find the grammatical or syntactical point that I had missed.

Their collective patience and diligence, imagination and attention to detail were both instructive and, invariably, both pointed and tactful.

Third in this triumvirate of advisors and advocates, critics, censors and cheerleaders, is Chuck Trainor. A long-time member of Siena's English faculty, Professor Trainor provided a careful and detached reading of the mss. which carefully noted both strengths and weaknesses. He isolated points which needed greater clarity, exposed incidents of literary excess. These and other felicities of editing resulted in a much tauter and more sensitive final draft.

Together with the two Dougs and Cris he is owed a huge debt for any strengths herein displayed. It is hereby acknowledged.

Obviously, any errors, solecisms or infelicities which remain are mine and mine alone.